Cell Phones and Distracted Driving

Other titles in the *Cell Phones and Society* series include:

Cell Phones and Teens
Cell Phones: Threats to Privacy and Security
How Do Cell Phones Affect Health?
How Do Cell Phones Affect Society?

Cell Phones and Society

Cell Phones and Distracted Driving

Gail B. Stewart

DISCARD

ReferencePoint
Press®

San Diego, CA

ReferencePoint
Press®

© 2015 ReferencePoint Press, Inc.
Printed in the United States

For more information, contact:
ReferencePoint Press, Inc.
PO Box 27779
San Diego, CA 92198
www.ReferencePointPress.com

LIBRARY OF CONGRESS CATALOGING-IN-PUBLICATION DATA

Stewart, Gail B. (Gail Barbara), 1949-
  Cell phones and distracted driving / by Gail B. Stewart.
    pages cm -- (Cell phones and society)
  Audience: Grade 9 to 12.
  Includes bibliographical references and index.
  ISBN 978-1-60152-642-7 (hardback) -- ISBN 1-60152-642-3 (hardback) 1. Distracted driving--Juvenile literature. 2. Cell phone calls--Juvenile literature. 3. Cell phones and traffic accidents--Juvenile literature. I. Title.
  HE5620.D59S83 2014
  363.12'51--dc23
                                                                        2013040173

9/15

Contents

Introduction   6
    Cell Phones Behind the Wheel

Chapter One   9
    The Distractions of Driving

Chapter Two   20
    The Science of Distraction

Chapter Three   32
    Cell Phones and the Law

Chapter Four   43
    Have Laws Reduced Cell Phone
    Distraction?

Chapter Five   53
    Other Efforts to Reduce Cell
    Phone Use by Drivers

Source Notes   63

Related Organizations and Websites   69

For Further Research   72

Index   74

Picture Credits   79

About the Author   80

Cell Phones Behind the Wheel

It was a somber morning on October 17, 2012, as 155 seniors and staff gathered in the commons area of the high school in the small town of Byron, Minnesota. Just seven weeks before, one of their own—seventeen-year-old senior Deianerah Logan (D.J. to her friends)—was killed when the van she was driving crashed into the back of a school bus that had stopped to drop off a second grader. The subsequent police investigation showed that the teen had been texting at the time she hit the bus.

"We Would Much Rather Be Grounding Her"

After learning that their daughter's inattentiveness had caused the accident, D.J.'s parents, Matt and Megan Logan, were determined that their tragedy would not be repeated with someone else's child. They asked to speak to D.J.'s fellow students about their loss and how a few moments of distracted driving had resulted in permanent heartbreak for their family. Standing together at the microphone, the Logans took turns reading a statement that they hoped would prevent D.J.'s schoolmates from making a similar mistake: "Seven weeks ago today, our daughter died in a tragic car accident. . . . You can imagine the details about our daughter's untimely death is devastating to our family, her friends and to those that knew D.J. Her error in judgment as a teenager in this brief moment in time was paid for with the highest price ever—her life. We would much rather be grounding her for this mistake than never hearing her laughter fill the house again."[1]

> "We would much rather be grounding her for this mistake than never hearing her laughter fill the house again."[1]
>
> —Matt and Megan Logan, parents of a Minnesota high school student killed while texting and driving.

Byron High School principal Mike Duffy vividly recalls the mood among the students as they listened to Matt and Megan Logan. "This wasn't like most assemblies at the high school," he says. "I mean, our students are pretty good, pretty respectful and they listen when we have a speaker, but that morning the kids were visibly hanging on every single word. They were reacting to the message, but as they watched D.J.'s mother and father fighting back tears, they were also reacting to the grief of the Logan family. The kids were fighting back their own tears. You could have heard a pin drop in there."[2]

In addition to speaking to the students, D.J.'s family passed out purple wristbands to the students to remind them of the dangers of using cell phones while driving. The district superintendent, Jeff Elstad, was impressed that the Logans were straightforward and honest about the way D.J. died. "It was a personal message from her parents to her classmates," Elstad said afterward. "They were very upfront about the findings of the investigation, and shared a touching message about how they want to be proactive."[3]

Accidents involving drivers distracted by their cell phones are increasing—and texting while driving is considered to be one of the biggest hazards on the road.

A Growing Problem

The tragic death of D.J. Logan is one of a growing number of horrific—though preventable—accidents occurring on roads and highways throughout the United States. More and more people are being injured and killed in accidents that are caused by drivers distracted by using their cell phones. As of June 2013, according to the National Safety Council (NSC), cell phone use was a factor in 21 percent of crashes nationwide. And in 2012 cell phone use by drivers was to blame for at least three thousand deaths, says the National Highway Traffic Safety Administration (NHTSA). Texting, specifically, is considered by experts to be one of the most dangerous aspects of cell phone use when driving, but having a conversation can be just as treacherous.

Life can change in an instant, says Moira Evans, a Chicago woman whose younger brother was severely injured in 2011 when a thirty-five-year-old man talking on his cell phone rear-ended his van:

> "Am I angry? Oh yes—I would love to ask that driver what phone call was so tremendously important that it couldn't have waited."[4]
>
> —Moira Evans, whose brother was critically injured by a driver talking on a cell phone.

It just is appalling what tragedy a few seconds on the phone can cause when that person should be driving. My brother did survive, and for that I am grateful, but he's being handed a different life altogether. It's not likely that he'll ever walk again. He has suffered severe head injuries and spinal trauma, and even today almost two years later, he's in constant pain. . . . Am I angry? Oh yes—I would love to ask that driver what phone call was so tremendously important that it couldn't have waited a moment or two until he could pull off the road and talk safely, instead of ruining someone else's life. I'd be very interested in his answer.[4]

The Logans might have asked the same question of their daughter, but it is a question that will never be answered. And as they told the Byron students, they hope that their daughter's error in judgment can make a difference in her classmates' lives. "She made a mistake, like all teenagers do, in the process of growing up," they said. "Except this time, there is no growing up. We can only pray that others can learn from her."[5]

The Distractions of Driving

Chapter One

Distracted driving occurs anytime a person engages in some activity that can interfere with the safe operation of a vehicle. According to a 2012 report by the NHTSA, 80 percent of crashes—as well as 65 percent of near crashes—involve some degree of driver distraction.

"The term 'distracted driving' hasn't been around all that long," says Lieutenant Eric Roeske, public information officer for the Minnesota State Patrol. "But distracted driving has been a problem since automobiles first took to the roads. We're using the term a lot more these days because we've got several advances in technology that just weren't around 20 or 30 years ago—including, but not limited to, cell phones. But no matter what the distraction, anything that takes your full attention from the road is a dangerous problem."[6]

Visual Distractions

To understand why cell phones rank at the top of the list of worrisome driving distractions, it is important to understand the way behavioral psychologists categorize human distractions. Visual distractions, for example, occur whenever a driver's eyes are diverted from the road. "A visual distraction inside the vehicle can be anything from looking in your bag or your purse for your sunglasses, or maybe a ringing cell phone," explains Minneapolis police officer Bradley Simonson. "Or you might be distracted by looking at a map or the car's GPS screen. That can take your eyes off the road—which we all know can lead to trouble. I say 'we all know,' but a lot of people forget that. We think we're just taking a quick peek, but we don't realize how fast something can develop on the street or highway that needs your full attention."[7]

It is not uncommon for young children in the car to cause parents to become visually distracted. Carley Schwartz, mother of two daughters, cites her reaction to her children's squabbling as the cause of her accident in 2009:

My girls—they were 3 and 6 at the time—were in the back of our minivan, and they were arguing about something, and it sort of escalated from name-calling to slapping at each other. They starting screaming and crying and all the noise was really getting to me. I kept looking in my rearview mirror, watching them and scolding them, and I got so distracted I rear-ended a pickup truck in front of me. The guy in the pickup had put on his brakes, but I never saw it until the very last minute. I did react, but not soon enough—I slammed into the back of his truck. Fortunately, no one was seriously hurt, but there was lots of damage to both of the vehicles. And I learned my lesson about trying to referee arguments while driving.[8]

Schwartz says that she is still bothered by nightmares from the ordeal. "I still feel that frantic, petrifying fear of not being able to brake in time," she says. "It's horrible, really. I've never felt something like that. I wake up screaming, my heart banging away inside my chest. I could have killed all of us that day, and the man in the truck ahead of me, too. You know, until you've made a terrible mistake like that, you have no idea how horrible you'll feel afterwards."[9]

Visual Distractions Outside the Vehicle

Visual distractions frequently occur outside the vehicle, too. Looking away to view an accident on the side of the road or a construction project or simply trying to read an address or a road sign can take a driver's eyes from the road for more than a second or two and possibly cause an accident.

One visual distraction that has gained a great deal of publicity is the digital billboard—a relatively new phenomenon but one that safety experts say has become the focus of concern. Unlike traditional billboards, digital billboards show lots of video and colorful, constantly changing images. In his 2010 article "Digital Billboards, Diversions Drivers Can't Escape," *New York Times* journalist Matt Richtel dubbed digital billboards as "television on a stick"[10] and noted that they are so eye-catching they could be dangerously distracting to drivers. "Images change every six to eight seconds," he writes, "so advertisers can flash timely messages—like the latest headlines, coffee deals at dawn, a cheeseburger at lunchtime or even the song playing on a radio station at that moment."[11]

The science seems to support Richtel's concern. A recent study by Virginia Tech for the National Highway Traffic Safety Administration found that anything that could take a driver's eyes from the road for more than two seconds at a time greatly increased the risk of a crash. A 2012 study by the Swedish Transport Administration concluded that digital billboards held drivers' attention for longer than the two-second limit—often distracting a driver's eyes for six seconds or more.

> "I wake up screaming, my heart banging away inside my chest. I could have killed all of us that day."[9]
>
> —Carley Schwartz, who caused an accident when distracted by her young daughters fighting in the backseat.

Physical Distractions

Another category of distraction is physical, which means that a driver is doing something with his or her hands other than keeping them on the steering wheel. For example, a recent survey by ExxonMobil found that 70 percent of Americans say that they eat while driving, while 83 percent say they drink beverages while behind the wheel.

Eating while driving is a potentially dangerous physical distraction. According to a 2012 study by the University of Leeds, the reaction time of drivers who were eating was up to 44 percent slower than drivers who were not. The reaction times of those who were sipping a beverage such as coffee or soda were more than 37 percent slower. "I bet the statistics don't show how terrible it is when you are driving and you spill a cup of hot coffee in your lap on the way to your job," says student Caaqil Iqbal. "I've done that, and you cannot help but lose your focus on driving. Your lap is burning, you are panicked because your work clothes are a mess. It is chaos. It happened to me just one time, but I would never risk that again. I'm just thankful that no one was near me on the road when it happened."[12]

Police have seen many physically distracted drivers—from men shaving and women applying makeup, to drivers eating lunch, holding a sandwich in one hand, a cup of soda in the other, and trying to steer with their knees. Police sergeant Kevin Rofidal of Edina, Minnesota, adds that lots of physical distractions can be more dangerous because

Although cell phones are a growing cause of distracted driving crashes, other distractions pose similar hazards. Among these are eating and drinking while driving.

they are often visually distracting, too. "For example," he says, "a guy who is shaving or a woman putting on makeup while driving—they've got their eyes occupied as well as their hands."[13]

Cognitive Distractions

The third type of distraction is cognitive, which means that a person's mind is simply not on driving. Instead, the driver might be thinking about a presentation he or she is going to give at work or worrying about an upcoming algebra exam. Roeske explains that drivers could have their hands on the steering wheel and their eyes on the road, but their attention could be entirely focused on something else:

> One common scenario is when you are daydreaming as you drive. It happens to everybody, I think—especially when you're driving on a very familiar route, like on the way to work. How many times have you finished driving that route, and you get to your destination and can't even remember the journey? You just sort of blank out. It's almost like you're on autopilot. And that can be very dangerous—you might have driven that route hundreds or even thousands of times, but if something unusual were to happen—you encounter road work, or the unexpected action of another vehicle—you just aren't going to react as fast. You can appear as though you're paying attention, but your mind is miles and miles away.[14]

Cognitive distractions can occur during an argument or any intense discussion; in fact, even thinking about stressful things can cause a driver to become distracted. A driver who has just had a disagreement with a supervisor at work, for example, might still be thinking about that exchange rather than concentrating on driving. While keeping both hands on the wheel and staring straight ahead, that driver is likely to be too cognitively distracted to be aware of the cars, bicyclists, or pedestrians in his or her path.

> "You just sort of blank out. It's almost like you're on autopilot."[14]
>
> —Eric Roeske of the Minnesota State Patrol.

Distracted Three Ways

Cell phone use is particularly dangerous because it can cause all three types of distraction. "If you're texting, your eyes and hands are on the phone, so that's physically and visually distracting," says Roeske. "And if you're talking, you're likely to be cognitively distracted—thinking about the conversation you're having, rather than what's happening around you."[15]

The statistics of traffic accidents involving cell phones reflect the level of distraction they cause. Drivers using cell phones results in an average of fifteen deaths and twelve hundred injuries each day in the United States, the Centers for Disease Control and Prevention (CDC) estimated in 2013. And the NSC singles out cell phone use as the cause of 21 percent of all crashes.

Texting is viewed as an especially dangerous cell phone distraction. According to the NHTSA, texting while driving is as much as six times more dangerous than driving while intoxicated—a statistic that would not surprise the relatives and friends of Debbie Dewniak of Colchester, Vermont. Dewniak was a victim of a texting teenage driver in 2012. One August evening of that year, as she was walking with her dog to get her mail, she was struck by a car when the texting driver veered off the road.

Dewniak was hit and carried for almost 20 yards (18.3 m) on the hood of the teen's car. Her injuries were life-changing. She suffered two broken arms, a shattered pelvis, and a broken leg, in addition to a torn thumb and numerous head injuries. Today her balance is poor, she has only limited use of her arms, and her speech is difficult to understand. She is completely dependent on her family for care. "She had her life planned, she was always planning everything," says her brother. "But now she can't plan anything, because she can't remember anything."[16]

Police say damage in accidents caused by a driver distracted by texting is often far more severe than in other types of accidents. That is because the unfortunate motorist or pedestrian in the path of a texting driver is likely to be hit at full speed. "There are no skid marks in a texting accident," explains police officer Misty Dailey of Elk Grove, California. "By the time the driver looks up, from the average 3–5 seconds their eyes are off the road, there is no reaction time to brake. Texting, alcohol, and any kind of drug that alters how a driver feels changes how a driver reacts to driving situations."[17]

Not Just Teens

Though teenagers are often mentioned as guilty of texting while behind the wheel, texting adult drivers actually outnumber them. In

Catching a Pizza, Breaking an Arm

One of the most common distractions that occur in the car is an object—a phone or a purse, for example—falling off the seat. Drivers who try to catch the falling object may become so distracted that they crash the car. But even a skilled NFL receiver is no match for driving distractions, as Detroit Lions wide receiver Nate Burleson found out on September 24, 2013, when he tried to catch two pizza boxes before they slid off the passenger seat of his SUV. In trying to prevent the pizzas from spilling, he hit a center median wall on the highway and broke his arm—shortening his season.

"Any time you're in a highway accident, there's potential for worse than broken bones," says Jim Schwartz, coach of the Lions. "I think we've all dealt with some sort of distraction driving before. . . . There's too many times I leave the office real late at night, and you grab something—and I've had it happen to me—drop it on your lap or do something else. That's stuff we all need to learn from."

Quoted in National Public Radio, "Lions WR Nate Burleson Breaks Arm in 1-Car Crash," September 24, 2013. www.npr.org.

2013 AT&T published a survey that found that 49 percent of adults admit that they text while driving even though they know it is wrong, while just 43 percent of teenagers admit that they text while driving. "I was a little bit surprised," says AT&T's Charlene Lake. "It was sobering to realize that [the rate of] texting by adults is not only high, it's really gone up in the last three years."[18]

The increase in adult texting and driving cannot be attributed to ignorance. Even with a blizzard of public service announcements reminding drivers about the dangers of texting, more and more adults are guilty of the practice. A Minnesota lab assistant named Kathleen (she asked that her last name not be used) says that she did not think much about texting until she bought a new cell phone. Since then, she confesses, texting has become almost an addiction—even when she is behind the wheel:

I never thought of myself as someone who would text and drive. But when I got my smartphone, it just seemed so much easier to text than it had been with my other cell phone, and I started texting to four or five of my friends on a regular basis. But it did get to be a problem. I always feel like I have to read a new incoming text, even if I was in traffic or if I'd already gone to bed. It's like it's impossible to ignore it. I've been lucky, so far—I haven't had an accident.[19]

Ignoring the Dangers

Twenty-one-year-old Texas college student Chance Bothe was not so lucky. In January 2012 Bothe was returning home from an early college class and was texting back and forth with a friend. Ironically, not only was Bothe aware of the dangers of texting and driving, his last text before his accident was the message "I need to quit texting, because I could die in a car accident."[20]

> "Texting by adults is not only high, it's really gone up in the last three years."[18]
>
> —Charlene Lake, a senior vice president of AT&T's public affairs division.

Just moments after sending the text, Bothe's car careened off a bridge and plunged 35 feet (10.7 m) into a ravine. He suffered more than a dozen broken bones—including a broken neck—as well as a face so badly injured that he required extensive reconstructive surgeries. He suffered brain injuries and had to relearn to speak and walk.

Bothe says that his ordeal made him realize how dangerous cell phone use is to a driver. "Don't do it," he says. "It's not worth losing your life. I went to my grandmother's funeral not long ago. And I kept thinking, it kept jumping into my head: 'I'm surprised that's not me up in that casket.' I came very close to that, to being gone forever."[21]

Drivers of Trucks, Buses, and Trains

Those drivers guilty of using cell phones are not just behind the wheel of automobiles. In fact, some of the most worrisome are those driving heavy vehicles such as large trucks, haulers of hazardous materials, and commercial buses. An accident caused by a distracted driver of a heavily loaded eighteen-wheel semi or a bus driver with thirty or more people aboard potentially involves far more risk to people than an accident with an automobile.

In 2010 a heavy-goods truck driver was texting while driving in South Yorkshire, England, and rear-ended a van, killing twenty-two-year-old pharmacy student Jemma O'Connell and severely injuring her boyfriend, Alan Godfrey. The sixty-seven-year-old driver of the truck had been sending text messages (one of which was 117 keystrokes long) as he was driving at 55 miles (88.5 kph) per hour. Because he was not watching the road, he slammed into Godfrey's van, causing a deadly domino effect as cars and trucks rammed into one another—and kept the busy motorway closed for more than six hours.

One of the most publicized instances of cell phone distraction in recent years involved a passenger train. On July 24, 2013, the driver

Accidents involving drivers distracted by their cell phones are increasing—and texting while driving is considered to be one of the biggest hazards on the road. This 2013 train crash in Spain reportedly happened when the train driver became distracted while using a cell phone.

Video Evidence of a Bus Driver Using a Cell Phone

In June 2013 in Berks County, Pennsylvania, a commercial bus driver was fired after a passenger took a video of him using one or more cell phones while driving. Miki Onwudinjo was one of fifteen passengers traveling from New York to Reading, Pennsylvania, on a Bieber Tourways bus. Onwudinjo, who was sitting in the front seat of the bus, used her cell phone to take a video of the driver. According to news reports, the three-minute video clearly showed the driver distracted by what appeared to be one device to his left, after which he pulled out a second phone—taking his hands off the wheel at times.

Onwudinjo explained later that she was very frightened by the driver's inattention: "I felt like I had to watch the road for him while I was recording. . . . The first thing that was running through my mind was like, 'OK, if this guy keeps doing this, I could die right now. . . . Here I am on a bus that weighs thousands and thousands of pounds and this man is utilizing two mobile devices going on a 45-mph highway."

Quoted in Ryan Hughes, "Bieber Bus Driver Takes Hands Off Wheel, Eyes Off Road to Use Cell Phone," WFMZ, June 4, 2013. www.wfmz.com.

of a train in Santiago de Compostela, Spain, was on a cell phone with the train's onboard ticket inspector just before the train derailed, killing seventy people and injuring sixty-six others. The driver was going almost twice the recommended speed when the crash occurred. It was the worst rail accident in Spain since the 1940s.

One passenger said the speed of the train did not worry him at first. "We didn't know what was the maximum speed, so I thought it was normal," he said. "And suddenly there was a curve, the suitcases fell, and everything went dark. And I hit my head a ton of times, and 10 seconds later I was wedged between seats, and I had people's legs on top of me."[22]

An investigation found that the driver, Francisco José Garzón Amo, had received several alerts that the train was going too fast and to reduce his speed. Just before the train derailed, it was going 119 miles per hour (191.5 kph) on a curve in the tracks—more than twice the recommended speed. Though in his trial he later claimed he had ended the call before the crash, the investigation contradicted Amo's story. He had been on the phone at the time of the derailment—a finding that added to growing anxiety that driver distraction is becoming all too common in vehicles of all sorts.

The Science of Distraction

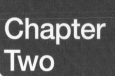

With the soaring rates of injuries and deaths caused by drivers distracted by cell phone use, it is not surprising that scientists and other researchers have been working to understand what causes the use of a cell phone to be so distracting. "It's not enough just to be intuitive about things like this," explains research technician Arthur Wouters. "You can say 'We think this process or this product is harmful or dangerous,' but you must be able to show data that supports your claim as to why it is so. . . . Data is the fuel that runs the machine."[23]

Early Research

There were some concerns about cell phones increasing the risk of crashes in the 1990s. Many of the first studies were statistical—meaning that researchers looked to see if there was a correlation between records of accidents and drivers' cell phone use.

In 1997 researchers at Sunnybrook Health Centre in Toronto, Canada, studied 699 drivers who had cell phones and who also had been involved in collisions during a fourteen-month period. After looking through nearly twenty-seven thousand detailed phone billing records that gave the time and duration of each call, researchers speculated that a driver on a cell phone had a risk of collision that was four times that of a driver not using a cell phone. One drawback of the study, however, is that no cause-and-effect data on collisions were included. In other words, scientists could not say for certain that cell phone use was the reason the accidents occurred.

One of the early experiments that looked at cell phone use as a cause of distraction took place at the University of Madrid in 2002. Scientists rode in cars with drivers and observed them while they were conversing (but not texting) on cell phones. The scientists found that drivers involved in conversations that required concentration had more trouble making driving decisions, noticing warning flashers, and controlling their speed. According to *Science News*, that study, which was released in 2002, "still stands as one of the clearest examples of what it means not to give full attention to the road."[24]

Driving and the Brain

Some of the most important research that has helped scientists understand distracted driving has focused not on cell phones but rather on the physical workings of a driver's brain. Paul Crawford, a senior research scientist for the Intel Interaction and Experience Research Lab, heads a team that is interested in learning more about distracted driving. His experiments have centered on driving behavior—not only where a driver is looking but also what that driver is thinking about when driving.

In one experiment Crawford demonstrated how he was able to measure the brain activity of a volunteer named Marvin. Marvin was sitting in a driving simulator connected to what looked much like a big-screen video game. Marvin was fitted with a headband containing an instrument called a functional near-infrared (fNIR) spectrometer, which measures activity in the outermost two centimeters of the brain.

In this case the fNIR spectrometer could tell when Marvin was focused on the task at hand or when he was distracted. "The functional near-infrared spectrometer measures your cognitive workload, or how hard your brain is working at processing information," Crawford explains. "With that information we can paint a picture of essentially the tasks you're dealing with mentally, and how challenging they are to you."[25]

In addition to the fNIR spectrometer, Crawford and his fellow researchers used cameras aimed at Marvin's eyes, measuring even the tiniest motions that took his attention off his driving. Anytime Marvin looked away for more than two seconds at a time, a timer went off, alerting Crawford. All of this data, including the activity in various parts of Marvin's brain as he was driving, was displayed on a monitor high above the game screen.

Researchers have been studying how distractions affect the brain. In some experiments, subjects sit in driving simulators similar to the one pictured here, while monitoring devices chart changes in brain activity as the driver masters various tasks.

Visible Distractions

At first Marvin played a relatively easy version of the driving game; at a speed of around 50 miles per hour (80 kph) he guided his car around the on-screen race track. Crawford noted that because very little was being asked of his brain, the fNIR spectrometer recorded very limited brain activity.

However, the second version was far more challenging, with speeds up to 250 miles per hour (402 kph). The displays of the fNIR spectrometer readings reflected a vast difference from the ones taken previously. Where the images of his brain were dark during the easy version of the game, in this challenging version large parts of his brain appeared bright yellow—highly active—on the display. To make

Marvin work even harder while his brain was engaged in the difficult driving, Crawford stood behind him while he drove and asked him to count backward from one hundred by sevens. While Marvin navigated the sharp turns, he had difficulty with the counting task, getting only to the first number—ninety-three—before making a mistake on the following number.

Crawford says that this kind of research explains a great deal about how engaged a person's brain is while doing a task that requires concentration. It is difficult for the brain to accomplish two tasks simultaneously that require high levels of concentration.

The Invisible Gorilla

Other research has focused on how people process what their eyes are seeing when they are engaged in an unrelated task. Scientists have been studying that idea since the 1990s, with the most groundbreaking work done by two Harvard psychologists, Dan Simon and Chris Chabris. Their experiment, known as "The Invisible Gorilla," was first conducted in 1999. This research was not specifically related to cell phone use. However, it validates the concept of "inattention blindness"—the idea that people frequently are unable to see what is right in front of their eyes when they are concentrating on something else. "The Invisible Gorilla" experiment has been replicated by dozens of other researchers around the world. One recent version of the experiment was conducted in 2011 at England's Hertfordshire University by psychology professor Richard Wiseman.

Wiseman begins the experiment by telling a group of volunteers that they are about to watch a video showing three men with yellow shirts running around in a gym passing a basketball back and forth. Wiseman tells the volunteers that their job is to count how many times the yellow-shirted men pass the basketball. He also explains that there are three men in the video wearing blue track suits, but there is no need to pay attention to them. The volunteers' only focus is on how many passes are made by the men in yellow.

As the volunteers begin watching the video, they silently keep track of the passes, just as they have been asked to do. About fifteen seconds into the video, an odd thing happens: A man in a gorilla suit and mask walks into the group of basketball players, faces the camera, thumps his chest, and slowly walks off camera. All the while, the men in yellow continue to pass the basketball.

When the video ends, the researcher asks the group how many passes they counted. The volunteers raise their hands to offer their answers. The researcher then asks if anyone noticed anything unusual in the video; only a few of the volunteers raise their hands.

Limits to the Brain's Attention

At this point in the experiment, the researcher asks the volunteers to watch the video again, but this time, they need not count passes. Instead, they should just watch it as they would a regular television program. Fifteen seconds into the video, as the gorilla makes its way into the midst of the athletes and looks at the camera, the volunteers erupt in laughter.

At the conclusion of the video, many of the volunteers who had not seen the gorilla the first time said they were stunned. One who had not noticed the gorilla in the first showing said he was somewhat leery of the results and wondered if the researcher had perhaps switched videos. Another volunteer admitted, "I'm embarrassed— I would have thought I could spot a monkey walking across the floor!"[26]

But researchers say that is just the point. When people are concentrating hard on something, they do not always see things around them. "Most of the time our vision does a wonderful job," explains Wiseman:

> But there's a limit to how much our brains can cope with. So we just pay attention to one thing at a time and wear blinds to the rest. The brain has a huge amount of information being delivered to it by the eyes. It has to make a decision—it has to decide where to place its attention, what information it should scrutinize, what information it should ignore. . . . Because [the volunteers] were all concentrating on counting, their brains just didn't register the gorilla.[27]

Learning the Hard Way

Jim Lutz, a Minneapolis salesman, says he learned the hard way that being distracted by his cell phone while driving could result in inattention blindness. In 2008 he was driving to a meeting and waiting to turn left at a stoplight: "It was busy at that time of day, morning rush hour traffic. I was on my phone with a client, and totally concentrating on what he was saying. And then I turned left, and didn't even see the woman who hit me! Didn't see her at all! She had the right of way, and I didn't. Simple as that. I was talking and so involved in my conversation I didn't even see her, though there was no reason for it. She was right in plain sight."[28] At the time of his accident, Lutz had never heard the term "inattention blindness," but now he understands the concept very well. "My eyes weren't involved because my brain wasn't, I guess is how I'd put it," he says. "I was looking, but I wasn't seeing. You'd think I'd have seen [that driver] coming. If I hadn't been having a phone conversation, I would have. I won't make that mistake again."[29]

Lutz's experience is not uncommon, researchers say. Research published in 2013 provides data that suggests why left-hand-turn accidents like Lutz's are fairly predictable when the driver is on a cell phone. In that study, neuroscientist Tom Schweizer of Toronto's St. Michael's Hospital and his team of researchers put a group of healthy young drivers in a high-powered magnetic resonance imaging (MRI) scanner that can evaluate in real time the workings of the various parts of the brain. The MRI was also equipped with a driving simulator with steering wheel, brake pedal, and accelerator. In this experiment the cell phones used were hands-free, so there was no physical distraction.

> "You'd think I'd have seen [that driver] coming. If I hadn't been having a phone conversation, I would have."[29]
>
> —Jim Lutz, insurance salesman.

Schweizer and his team also involved the test subjects in a conversation meant to distract them while they were driving—asking them a series of true or false questions. As they listened to and answered the questions, there was a significant amount of reduction in activity in the part of the brain that controls vision. At the same time, the part of the brain involved in having a conversation was activated.

Though the subjects were asked to do a variety of maneuvers during the questioning, it was left-hand turns that showed the most significant changes in the MRI. As the subjects answered the researchers' questions on their cell phone, the MRI showed the blood move from the visual cortex—the part of the brain that controls sight—to the prefrontal cortex, which is important in decision making.

According to Schweizer, with or without the distraction of a cell phone, the task is more difficult than most. "Visually, a left-hand turn is quite demanding," he explains. "You have to look at oncoming traffic, pedestrians and lights, and coordinate all that. Add talking on a cell phone, and your visual area shuts down significantly, which obviously is key to performing the maneuver."[30]

The Distraction of Listening

Other researchers have attempted to pinpoint the precise reason or reasons that cell phone use in particular is so distracting. In one study scientists at Carnegie Mellon University used brain imaging to prove that merely listening to someone talking on a cell phone can be an enormous distraction that leads to potentially dangerous driving mistakes. In this study, led by neuroscientist Marcel Just, researchers used brain imaging to monitor twenty-nine volunteers who took turns inside an MRI. The MRI was fitted with a driving simulator that allowed volunteers to drive on a virtual winding road at a challenging speed—meaning that to drive safely, it required close attention. The MRI kept track of minute changes in brain activity. While driving the simulator, some of the volunteers used a cell phone to answer a series of questions that required true or false answers. Other volunteers drove uninterrupted. The MRI measured changes in brain activity in both groups every second.

The results of the study showed two interesting things. First, Just and his team noted a big difference in the amount of brain activity between the two groups. Those who were listening to the true-false questions on their cell phones showed significant changes in the parietal and occipital lobes, the parts of the brain that are associated with driving. The parietal lobe processes sensory information such as navigation and spatial relationships. The occipital lobe is key to pro-

Passenger Conversation Versus Cell Phone Conversation

A number of studies have measured levels of driver distraction in different scenarios. These studies have shown that a driver who converses with a passenger does not experience nearly the level of distraction as a driver who talks on a cell phone. Scientists have several theories that might help to explain these results. One theory suggests that a passenger will probably stop talking to the driver if road conditions become potentially dangerous (for example, in connection with weather or traffic flow). A person on the other end of a cell phone conversation, however, will not have this information and will continue talking to the driver regardless of what is happening on the road. Another theory is that when talking on a cell phone, people tend to visualize the person on the other end of the conversation—something that a driver does not have to do with a passenger in the car. "When we communicate with a person we can't see, we create a mental image of them," says Clifford Nass, a sociologist at Stanford University. Such visualization takes brain power away from the more immediate task of driving safely.

Interestingly, the more remote the conversation is, the more taxing it is on the driver. In one experiment taking place in California, Nass's team told some drivers that the person on the other end of the cell phone was calling from nearby and other drivers that the call was coming from Chicago. The voice was identical, says Nass, but "people drove significantly worse when they thought it was from Chicago."

Quoted in Nathan Seppa, "Impactful Distraction: Talking While Driving Poses Dangers That People Seem Unable to See," *Science News,* August 9, 2013. www.sciencenews.org.

cessing visual information. In those sections of the brain, the MRI found a 37 percent reduction of activity in the group that was using cell phones while driving. The second finding of the Carnegie Mellon study was the remarkable deterioration in the driving skills of the participants who were listening to the questions on their cell phones. That group committed more driving errors such as deviating from the middle of their lane and even hitting simulated guardrails.

These results were surprising to the researchers. They believed that because driving and listening were two very different brain tasks, subjects' brains would be able to handle the rigors of driving and listening simultaneously. But Just explained later that their study illustrates that the brain can only do so much at one time, even though the two tasks involved two different brain networks.

The two parts of the brain that play an essential role in driving are the parietal and occipital lobes. The parietal lobe (green, upper right) processes sensory information such as navigation and spatial relationships; the occipital lobe (blue, lower right) processes visual information.

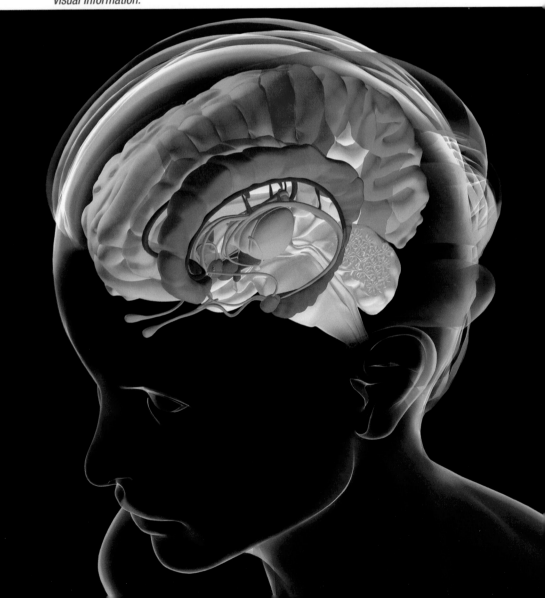

Cell Phone Chat and Drunk Driving

Some of the most groundbreaking research on the dangers of cell phone use by drivers was done by David Strayer, a cognitive psychologist at the University of Utah. Strayer and his team have done studies involving a number of research methods, including using sophisticated driving simulators that look and feel much like a real car—unlike many studies that use simulators that do not resemble a real car. He has studied the responses of people "driving" in these more realistic simulators—some using cell phones, others not.

His research found that talking or texting on a cell phone seriously impairs driving. A driver who is talking on a cell phone is four times more likely to have an accident than a driver who is not talking on a cell phone. And texting and driving doubles that risk. Strayer notes that talking on a cell phone and driving carries the same crash risk as driving drunk and that texting and driving represents an even greater hazard than driving drunk. "For comparison purposes, someone who is drunk at a .08 blood alcohol level has a four-time crash increase," Strayer explains. "So talking on a cell phone is about the same as driving drunk. When you're text messaging, the crash risk goes up eight times."[31]

> "Talking on a cell phone is about the same as driving drunk. When you're text messaging, the crash risk goes up eight times."[31]
>
> —*University of Utah psychologist David Strayer.*

The Myth of Multitasking

Strayer teamed with a University of Utah colleague, psychology professor David Sanbonmatsu, to investigate other issues that relate to cell phone use and driving. One of these pertains to multitasking. Many people believe they can safely multitask behind the wheel, but experts say most drivers have an inflated view of their ability to drive safely and talk or text on a cell phone.

The study by Strayer and Sanbonmatsu was published in January 2013. It ran 310 psychology students through a series of questionnaires to learn how they perceived their ability to multitask. The questionnaires also measured personality traits such as impulsivity and sensation seeking. The students ranked their own perceived multitasking ability on a scale of one to one hundred and

Teens, Cell Phones, and Risky Behavior

A 2012 CDC study found that teenagers who text while behind the wheel are also more likely to engage in other risky behaviors—including riding with an intoxicated driver and choosing not to wear a seatbelt. In the study the CDC found that four out of nine high school students admitted to having sent or received texts while driving during the previous month. CDC statistician Emily Olsen and her team analyzed responses to the agency's annual youth risk survey. In that survey 8,505 high school students sixteen and older were asked about potentially hazardous driving situations during the previous thirty days. Slightly under 45 percent admitted to having texted while driving during that time frame, while 12 percent said that they texted while driving every day.

According to researchers, the more often students reported texting while driving, the more likely those students were to answer "yes" when asked about other risky behaviors. For instance, 19 percent of those teens who admitted texting and driving at least once in the previous thirty days also admitted driving after drinking alcohol, whereas only 3 percent of teens who did not text while driving had driven after drinking alcohol.

Olsen says that those statistics are worrisome. "It's concerning that kids are participating in these multiple behaviors, either while driving or while they're a passenger," she says. "Each one of these things is quite dangerous [on its own]."

Quoted in Genevra Pittman, "Teens Who Text While Driving Likely to Engage in Other Risky Behaviors," *News-Herald* (Lake County, OH), August 8, 2013. www.news-herald.com.

provided information about how often they use a cell phone while driving.

In another part of the study, Strayer and Sanbonmatsu put each student in sophisticated driving simulators that looked and handled remarkably like real automobiles. While driving, the students were given a test called Operation Span, or OSPAN. The test measures the ability to answer simple computation questions as well as to keep several items in one's head at the same time.

The results of the study surprised the scientists. The subjects who did best on the OSPAN test while driving indicated on their questionnaires that they were less likely to multitask while driving. Those subjects who rated themselves on the questionnaires as skilled multitaskers, on the other hand, performed worse on the driving simulator tests. That group also tested very high for being risk takers and impulsive. According to Sanbonmatsu, "What is alarming is that people who talk on cell phones while driving tend to be the people least able to multitask well. Our data suggest the people talking on cell phones while driving are people who probably shouldn't."[32]

Research has repeatedly demonstrated the hazards of multitasking behind the wheel. Even so, the numbers of accidents, fatalities, and injuries continue to grow, and there is no indication that drivers will give up the use of their cell phones voluntarily.

"Our data suggest the people talking on cell phones while driving are people who probably shouldn't."[32]

—University of Utah psychologist David Sanbonmatsu.

Cell Phones and the Law

Chapter Three

The overwhelming conclusion of most scientific studies is that talking or texting on a cell phone while driving is a safety hazard. This presents a quandary for lawmakers who understand that, despite the potential risks, cell phones are considered an essential piece of technology in modern life. Almost 91 percent of adults and 78 percent of teens own and use a cell phone, according to a 2013 Pew Research poll. Pew Research describes cell phones as "the most quickly adopted consumer technology in the history of the world."[33]

Not surprisingly, some legislators are reluctant to be on the record in support of limitations to cell phone use. Many of their constituents resent any government agency—whether federal, state, or local—passing laws that limit their right to use their cell phone wherever they like. "I don't like the idea of it at all," says Texas resident Louisa McIntyre: "My opinion is that government should just stay out of things like what people do in their own cars. I know very well that I can use a cell phone and drive without having an accident. I'm careful, and I use common sense. . . . I don't believe we need politicians to tell us what to do in our own cars with the phone we paid for. . . . See, this is what people mean when they talk about the 'nanny state'—the government is trying to take care of us like we're a bunch of kindergarteners."[34]

The idea of personal freedom is ingrained in the American way of life, but not all Americans share the view that laws represent an infringement on that freedom. Some laws are needed for the overall public good because people are not always strong enough or insightful enough to act rationally—or safely—and their actions might endanger not only themselves but others. This is the view of Marcie Rivera, a Michigan health care worker, who says, "The way I see it, right now the notion of common sense is taking a backseat to technology. It seems every week or so the news leads with some gruesome accident caused by someone on a cell phone. Often a child or a teenager is killed. There just has to be a way to get drivers to hang up and pay attention to what they're supposed to be doing."[35]

Different States, Different Laws

Though the issue is controversial, the growing numbers of injuries and deaths caused by drivers distracted by cell phone use have resulted in most states passing restrictions limiting their use. A few states—including Arkansas, California, Connecticut, Delaware, and Maryland—have banned handheld cell phone use by drivers, though use of hands-free devices are permissible. Other states ban cell phone use for drivers in particular categories, such as novice drivers under eighteen years of age or school bus drivers.

As of October 2013 the banned category on which the most states agree is that of texting. All but three states have banned texting—either for all drivers or for at least one category, such as bus drivers or novice drivers. For example, though Alaska has no ban on handheld cell phone use for talking while driving, its state legislature has banned all texting while driving. And in Missouri, drivers under twenty-one are prohibited from texting while driving, but older drivers can legally text or talk while driving.

In some instances cities have enacted their own bans on the use of cell phones while driving—even though the state itself has none. For example, Texas has no statewide law banning the use of cell phones while driving, but twenty-two cities have enacted laws banning the practice, including Galveston, El Paso, and Austin. In Arizona no talking or texting bans exist statewide, but within the city limits of Phoenix and Tucson texting is banned.

"It can be a nightmare," says salesman Mike Pfiefer, who travels by car extensively in the western United States. "I do tend to use my cell phone a lot when I drive—when it's legal. But that's the problem, it's hard to keep track of exactly where you are, legal-wise. You can be fine on the highway in Texas, but you get into a particular city like Galveston, San Antonio, or Austin and it's like the troopers are just waiting for you. A lot of the time you don't see a sign to warn you that you're in one of those cities, and there's like six or seven of them."[36]

An electronic freeway sign reminds California drivers that using a handheld cell phone while driving is illegal. Laws on cell phone use while driving vary widely from state to state.

Forces Behind Cell Phone Laws

Cell phone laws are not always enacted for the same reason. Politicians may hear from their constituents that they want some regulation, but one of the most powerful forces behind legislation is the well-publicized death of a victim of distracted driving—often a child or teenager. One example is nine-year-old Erica Forney of Fort Collins, Colorado, whose death in 2008 was a strong motivation for Colorado lawmakers to limit cell phone use by drivers. On November 25 Erica was riding her bicycle home from school. She was only two houses from home when she was hit head-on by a Ford Expedition SUV. The woman behind the wheel had looked down at her cell phone as she finished a call and never saw Erica. As her car swerved into the bicycle lane, the little girl was thrown 15 feet (4.6 m), landing on her neck.

Shelly Forney, Erica's mother, says her daughter was rushed to the area children's hospital and soon afterward was airlifted to another facility. "The neurosurgeon made it very clear that she was going to die," she says. "I spent the night with her. . . . I held her. Cried. I kissed her. I sang to her. I just needed to have time with my girl."[37]

At the time, Colorado had no ban on texting or talking on cell phones. After the accident the Forneys began working hard to change Colorado's laws. "I don't want any other parent to have to go through this, or a husband to lose his wife,"[38] Shelly says.

When the law was passed, Colorado governor Bill Ritter traveled to Fort Collins to sign it. "Driving requires our full attention," Ritter announced in a statement. "Drivers should not be texting while behind the wheel. And drivers younger than 18 ought to be focusing on the road, not their cellphones."[39]

> "I spent the night with her. . . . I held her. Cried. I kissed her. I sang to her. I just needed to have time with my girl."[37]
>
> —*Shelly Forney, mother of a nine-year-old girl who was killed by a driver talking on her cell phone.*

Taylor's Law

Heeding Ritter's advice might well have saved the life of eighteen-year-old college student Taylor Sauer of Caldwell, Idaho. She was killed on January 12, 2012, as she was making the four-hour drive home from Utah State University. Along the way she was texting a friend on Facebook, talking about the Denver Broncos football team. Eerily, her last text was, "I can't discuss this now. Driving and Facebook is not safe! Haha!"[40]

Just a few moments later, her car slammed into the back of a slow-moving tanker truck as it went up a hill. Taylor was going eighty miles per hour and was killed instantly. And like so many other accident scenes in which cell phones are involved, investigators found no skid marks—no signs that the teen had tried to stop. Later, the same investigators examined her cell phone records and saw that she had been posting approximately every ninety seconds during the drive. "The text messages were both incoming and outgoing during her trip between Logan, Utah and [the accident scene]," explains Idaho State Police lieutenant Sheldon Kelley. "In addition to the texting, there were multiple Facebook communications to and from Taylor Sauer during the minutes immediately prior to the crash."[41]

After their daughter's death, Clay and Shauna Sauer worked to toughen the penalties and strengthen the laws on distracted driving. They testified before Idaho's state legislature during its consideration of a texting-while-driving ban. Though the bill had been voted down before, it passed in 2012. Lawmakers attributed the law's passage to the emotional testimony of the Sauer family.

Utah's Texting Law

As in Idaho, Utah's cell phone law was influenced by tragedy on the highway. On the rainy morning of September 22, 2006, James Furaro and Keith O'Dell were driving to work along a two-lane highway west of Logan, Utah. Both worked at ATK Launch Systems, designing and building rocket boosters. A nineteen-year-old college student and part-time painter, Reggie Shaw, was driving west along the same highway. As he drove he was exchanging text messages with his girlfriend. His car drifted across the center line, just clipping the Saturn driven by Furaro and sending the car careening into the path of a pickup truck hauling a trailer packed with nearly 2 tons (1.8 metric tons) of horseshoes and blacksmith equipment. Furaro and O'Dell were killed instantly.

> "I can't discuss this now. Driving and Facebook is not safe! Haha!"[40]
>
> —Taylor Sauer, killed in a car accident just moments after sending this text.

Shaw initially denied doing anything that could have caused his car to swerve into the other lane. However, after a witness came forward and said that he had seen Shaw's car weaving shortly before the crash, the investigating officer got a court order to subpoena Shaw's cell phone records. They showed that he had sent or received a total of eleven texts in the minutes leading up to the crash. Shaw then admitted that he had been texting.

Shaw was sentenced to serve thirty days in jail, to complete two hundred hours of community service, and to read Victor Hugo's *Les Misérables* for inspiration on how to make a significant contribution to society. However, Utah lawmakers were determined that anyone who texts and causes injury or death needs a far harsher punishment. Under the law passed in 2009, any motorist caught texting faces up to three months in jail and up to a $750 fine. However, if a texting

People Who Text Drivers May Be Liable

New Jersey lawmakers have tried a different tactic in efforts to stop people from texting and driving. A law adopted in 2013 states that a person who knowingly texts someone who is driving can be held liable if the driver is involved in a crash that is connected with texting.

The case that inspired the new law involved eighteen-year-old Kyle Best, who was driving while texting with his girlfriend, seventeen-year-old Shannon Colonna, in September 2009. Just seconds after he sent her a text message, his truck veered across the center line and slammed head-on into a motorcycle carrying David and Linda Kubert. Both riders were critically injured. The prosecuting attorney suggested that in a way, Colonna was in the car—although just electronically—and as a result should be held accountable for the accident, too.

In this particular case, however, it could not be proved that Colonna knew that her boyfriend was driving at the time she was texting him. But the New Jersey Appeals Court ruled that in the future, the sender of a text message can potentially be liable if it can be proved that the texter knew that the person to whom the text was sent was driving.

motorist causes injury or death, it is categorized as a felony, resulting in a fine of up to $10,000 and fifteen years in jail.

Beefing Up Existing Cell Phone Laws

In some cases state laws addressing the use of cell phones by drivers have become stricter by becoming more specific. In Virginia, for example, though texting while driving has been illegal since 2009, the practice was considered a secondary offense. That means that the law permitted police to issue a ticket only if the driver had been stopped for another infraction, such as speeding. In 2012, however, Virginia's legislature voted to change cell phone use to a primary offense. "Now, with it being a primary offense," says Frederick County deputy sheriff Warren Gosnell, "simply seeing a person doing something with their phone other than a phone call, which the code states, a non–phone call use: email, text, Facebook, Twitter, anything besides actually making a call . . . is now a primary offense. Meaning I can stop you, investigate and take action if necessary."[42]

Besides reclassifying cell phone use behind the wheel, some states have added stiffer penalties for texting or talking on cell phones. For example, Illinois passed a law in August 2013 against talking or texting on handheld cell phones; the law increased the fine from twenty to seventy-five dollars for the first offense, and the fine increases with each subsequent violation. In addition, the Illinois law classifies cell phone use behind the wheel as a moving violation. That means drivers who get three tickets in a year find themselves in danger of losing their license. "The only way to correct such a bad habit is to have a law with teeth in it," explains Illinois state representative John D'Amico. "So people are gonna think twice after they get that one ticket. I think that's a pretty hefty fine."[43]

No state, however, has fines and punishments as severe as those in Alaska. As of May 2012 a motorist caught texting could face up to a year in jail and a fine up to $10,000. According to Alaska state representative Les Gara, who led the move for the law, it was crucial to ban a very dangerous activity: "The Legislature intended to ban dangerous conduct like texting while driving. . . . We're sending a clear message to the public, now, that texting and typing on personal and computer devices can cause death and serious injury. In an average text you drive the length of a football field before paying attention to driving. We don't want cars to be moving weapons."[44]

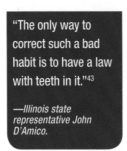

"The only way to correct such a bad habit is to have a law with teeth in it."[43]

—Illinois state representative John D'Amico.

Are Laws Necessary?

But not every state has chosen to limit drivers' cell phone use. Arizona lawmakers, for example, have only banned school bus drivers from texting while driving. Some of those Arizonans in opposition to limiting the use of cell phones insist that drivers must be allowed to make their own decisions. Others, such as Arizona governor Jan Brewer, have maintained that such laws would not be effective. "You can write all the laws you want," she says. "But it sometimes doesn't make a whole lot of difference. People don't follow them."[45]

Signs of Grief

When Mike Kellenyi's eighteen-year-old daughter Nikki died in an accident believed to have been caused by a cell phone–distracted driver, he pushed for
a law requiring more signs to warn motorists about using their phones while
driving. Kellenyi wanted his daughter's legacy to be a reminder to motorists that
texting while driving is illegal in New Jersey. Nikki's Law, as it is called, requires
New Jersey's Department of Transportation to erect more signs reminding motorists that texting is illegal—hopefully saving other families from the grief the
Kellenyi family had experienced.

In commenting on the law, Assemblyman Paul D. Moriarty notes:

Nikki's death shook our community quite a bit. Over 4,000 members of
our community came out to her funeral, and last week, there was another
vigil—over 500 people showed up to remember the night of her death.
Nikki was buried in the prom dress she never got to wear, holding the
prom ticket she never got to use.

Her death reminds us of the danger of inattentive driving and it reminds
us of the need to continue to educate the public throughout our state and
throughout the country to put down the phones, put down the distractions and pay attention.

Quoted in New Jersey Assembly Democrats, "New Jersey Democrats Raising Awareness of the
Dangers of Distracted Driving," news release, May 8, 2013. www.assemblydems.com.

Arizona senator Steve Farley, who has introduced a number of
bills banning texting, disagrees. Citing scientific studies about the
increased risk of accidents while using a cell phone, he says it far
surpasses the dangers of other driver distractions and thus needs its
own law. Texting while driving "is so far out there as a danger [more]
than anything else—eating a burger, putting on makeup, anything
else—it deserves to be called out as a specific practice that needs to be
banned,"[46] he insists.

Vinnie Sorce, a software tester in Chino Valley, Arizona, agrees
wholeheartedly with Farley. Sorce has a personal stake in the issue.

The wreckage of a 2008 collision between a commuter train and a freight train in Chatsworth, California, illustrates the distraction posed by texting. An investigation revealed that the commuter train engineer missed warnings about switching tracks because he was texting while driving.

His fiancé, Stacey Stubbs, was killed in a 2007 crash when a teenager who was texting struck her car. Since then Sorce has been advocating for a ban on texting while driving but admits he is tired of fighting with people who don't understand. "I can't stand to see people arguing over it," he explains. "I got tired of trying to convey it to people; nobody seemed to be listening."[47]

Federal Laws

Traffic laws, including those that deal with cell phones and driving, are usually the responsibility of state legislatures. However, some of the recent laws limiting drivers' use of cell phones were enacted by the US Department of Transportation under former secretary Ray LaHood. In 2011 LaHood announced a ban on handheld cell phone use by the nation's more than 4 million interstate or commercial truck and bus drivers. "When drivers of large trucks, buses, and hazardous materials take their eyes off the road for even a few seconds, the outcome can be deadly," LaHood says. "I hope this rule will save lives by helping commercial drivers stay laser-focused on safety at all times behind the wheel."[48]

The penalty for those who violate the law is a fine of up to $2,750 for each offense. A driver who commits multiple offenses risks losing his or her license to operate a commercial vehicle. The reaction from the trucking industry was largely negative. Andres Eisenbiess of Gully Transportation insists that cell phones are a must for a truck driver, and to ban their use while driving could make the roads less safe. "Drivers use cell phones to call in wrecks, DUI cases, stranded motorists, and . . . to keep in touch with their fellow drivers and stay in touch with their family when they're out on the road."[49]

No Cell Phones for Railroad Engineers

Though most of the laws limiting cell phone use involve motor vehicles, some have addressed other forms of transportation. In 2010, for example, the Federal Railroad Administration (FRA) adopted a new prohibition on cell phone use by train operators. That ban was prompted by a collision between a Metrolink commuter train and a Union Pacific freight train in Chatsworth, California, in 2008—the worst accident in Metrolink history. Twenty-five people died in that crash, including Metrolink engineer Robert Sanchez, and 135 were injured. An investigation by the National Transportation Safety Board found that Sanchez had ignored signals and warnings that it was unsafe for him to proceed onto a single-track section. Sanchez missed the warnings because he had been texting on his cell phone. He did not slow down, and as a result the Metrolink train was going 40 miles per hour (64 kph) when it was hit head-on by the freight train—also going 40 miles per hour. The impact occurred twenty-two seconds after Sanchez's last text.

FRA administrator Joseph Szabo describes the dangers of distracted driving as far too serious to allow engineers and others entrusted with the safety of the public to use cell phones on the job:

"Distracted driving is an epidemic. It is dangerous, deadly, and irresponsible when operating any type of transportation equipment. That's why we have banned the unauthorized use of electronic devices while operating freight or passenger trains and why many railroads also have adopted strict operating rules against the practice."[50]

The various laws passed to limit or curtail cell phone use by drivers have been a cause for optimism by safety experts. And yet the number of deaths and injuries resulting from distracted driving accidents has not diminished but grown—a fact that has perplexed the safety experts.

Have Laws Reduced Cell Phone Distraction?

In 2009 the *New York Times* ran a four-part series calling attention to the extent of the problem of cell phones and distracted driving. Since that time, there has been a flurry of new legislation regulating the use of cell phones by motorists. As of September 2013 laws limiting at least some aspect of cell phone use have been passed by forty-seven states, and forty-one states and the District of Columbia have banned texting while driving.

However, statistics show that the roads are no safer. According to the NHTSA, 3,331 deaths are known to have been caused by distracted drivers in 2011—the most recent year for which statistics are available. This number represents an increase over 2010, when the death toll in connection with distracted driving reached 3,261. According to the NHTSA, 12 percent of the 2011 deaths were specifically caused by cell phone distraction.

The Governors Highway Safety Association (GHSA) is a nonprofit consortium that represents the highway safety offices of all fifty states. A study by the GHSA released in 2013 found that only eleven states say their distracted-driving crashes have decreased since the adoption of laws limiting cell phone use by motorists, while thirty-one states say the rate of crashes has either increased or stayed the same as before the laws were passed.

Are Cell Phone–Related Accidents Underreported?

Despite all of the recent publicity about the dangers of cell phone use while driving, some researchers believe that the public may not be aware of how prevalent cell phone–related accidents have become. One likely reason for this, experts say, is that statistics of deaths and injuries caused by cell phone distraction are vastly underreported. Anytime there is a traffic accident resulting in a fatality, police code the information into the Fatal Analysis Reporting System, maintained by the

NHTSA. That database helps experts keep track of the causes of fatalities—from drunk driving or speeding to falling asleep at the wheel or using a cell phone. This information helps the NHTSA monitor trends in driving behavior.

But in a study released in 2013 by the NSC, researchers found evidence that deadly accidents involving cell phone–distracted drivers had not been properly coded in the database. The researchers looked at 180 fatal crashes that occurred nationwide between 2009 and 2011 in which there was compelling evidence that cell phone use had been a cause. They found that only 52 percent of those cases were subsequently entered as cell phone related. "We believe the number of crashes involving cell phone use is much greater than what is being reported," notes Janet Froetscher, president of the NSC. "Many factors—from drivers not admitting cell phone use, to a lack of consistency in crash reports being used to collect data at the scene—make it very challenging to determine an accurate number."[51]

> "The number of crashes involving cell phone use is much greater than what is being reported."[51]
>
> —Janet Froetscher, president of the National Safety Council.

Difficulty in Enforcement

The difficulty of enforcing laws that limit or ban cell phone use by drivers has also called into question the success of such laws. Police in states that have enacted texting and driving bans say that catching drivers in the act is not as easy as it sounds. The challenge is compounded by the large numbers of people who ignore the laws.

While it is far easier for a driver to text with the phone at eye level—usually resting against the steering wheel—many drivers frequently keep the phone below window level as they text. That makes it almost impossible for a police officer to spot them entering messages into the keypad. Bradley Simonson says that many drivers—especially teenagers—are proficient at typing texts without glancing at their phones: "It's really amazing how well a lot of people—especially teenagers—can type their texts without even looking at the phone in their lap. I've watched my daughter text at home—her fingers just click across the keypad, she doesn't look down at all. I mean, I couldn't do it,

Police officers say drivers have become adept at hiding their texting behavior while on the road, making it difficult to identify those who are violating the law. A series of photos, taken in 2013 in Toronto, Canada, illustrates this problem.

but I guess kids are more used to it. So for us, a driver who is texting with the phone down below window level is a lot less obvious than one who's got the phone up near the steering wheel."[52]

Legal Confusion

Sometimes the laws themselves are confusing, making enforcement almost impossible. For example, Virginia law makes it illegal "to manually enter multiple letters or texts while driving or to read any email or text messages that have been transmitted to the device."[53] However, the law permits drivers to use their hands to make cell phone calls or to use their smartphones to access the GPS. Virginia defense attorney Greg Sheldon says it is virtually impossible for a police officer to tell whether a driver is checking the GPS or texting. "I don't know how you would train an officer to look for somebody manually entering multiple letters or texting," he says. "It may look like I'm manually entering text, but I may be putting

The Importance of "Me"

One of the reasons cited by experts to explain why people continue to use cell phones while they drive—even when it is illegal—is that people feel that their conversations are too important to put off. In the following excerpt from an editorial, Mark Borgard, editor of the *Kingman Daily Miner*, explains his frustration with such drivers.

We just don't care about other people. Our lives are much more important than theirs. We're big shots. We drive big trucks, make a lot of money, live fascinating lives. We don't have time to pay attention to the road while we're driving. We figure that if we get in an accident, odds are our elite status, coupled with our financial security, will pretty much get us out of any scrape. . . .

I would love to buy a paint gun and tag the cars driven by people on cell phones, but I save that for my daydreams, because I would certainly end up in jail, or worse, cause the very accident I'm trying to avoid. . . . You may have noticed by now I've said nothing about texting while driving. That is so stupid it doesn't deserve attention. If you text while driving, you're an idiot. Your luck will run out eventually. I just pray it doesn't run out when you're next to me on the road.

Mark Borgard, "Your Cell Phone Use Is Driving Me Crazy," *Kingman (AZ) Daily Miner*, January 3, 2010.

in a phone number and, under the statute, I can use my phone in my car."[54]

Police officer Greg Tyson of Savannah-Chatham, Georgia, encountered this problem in 2010, shortly after Georgia passed a no-texting law. He says it was difficult to determine whether motorists he was observing were breaking the law. If he could not actually see a cell phone in a driver's hand, he did not have probable cause to pull the driver over unless the driver was swerving or driving in some other reckless manner that indicated he or she was distracted. When Tyson finally did see a woman driving with her cell phone in hand, she informed Tyson that she had not been texting but rather had been checking directions on her phone's GPS. Short of checking the cell phone history, which is not legal in many states without a warrant, police have few options for proving or disproving a motorist's story.

A Sense of Invincibility

Drivers who ignore cell phone laws know that there is little chance of getting caught. And many simply believe they are not at risk. While scientific research has clearly shown that driving while using a cell phone increases the chances of a crash, many drivers believe that they are more than capable of handling both tasks at once.

Retired California businessman Jeff Chaney is one such driver. He admits that he has been ticketed once for texting while behind the wheel, but the officer acknowledged that Chaney had not been weaving out of his lane or driving dangerously. "He said I was flagrantly texting," Chaney says. "I was completely in control of my car. I was texting my daughter to tell her I was going to be late getting to her house, and I thought it was a waste of time to pull onto a rest stop [on the highway] just to send a text. I am old enough and smart enough to know my limitations. If I thought I was a danger or a menace to others, I wouldn't text. I know what I'm doing."[55]

Experts say that the problem is not that lawbreakers are ignorant of the risks, either. In fact, a 2011 survey by the American Automobile Association (AAA) found that 87 percent of people know that texting while driving is dangerous, yet 20 percent admit to doing it anyway. According to the AAA's Foundation for Traffic Safety, nine out of ten Americans understand that talking on the phone while driving poses a substantial danger, yet seven out of ten admit to checking their text messages and e-mails while behind the wheel.

Researchers believe that one of the reasons people feel invincible when it comes to driving while using a cell phone is because they have not yet had an accident. In fact, with the large percentage of drivers

> "For us, a driver who is texting with the phone down below window level is a lot less obvious than one who's got the phone up near the steering wheel."[52]
>
> —Bradley Simonson, police officer.

who admit to using cell phones, one might expect the fatality and injury rates to be far higher. University of Kansas psychologist Richard Atchley says that because driving is boring and uneventful, most of the time drivers get away with these lapses of attention while using their cell phones. Notes Atchley, "[That's why] it's hard to explain why talking is dangerous."[56]

Some psychologists say that along with the sense of invincibility, many drivers (especially young drivers) are used to doing several things at once. They simply do not see that driving and texting is any different from, say, simultaneously doing homework and watching a YouTube video. Researcher Clifford Nass of Stanford University says that may explain why young drivers who have been raised on electronic gadgets like cell phones are less willing to give them up while behind the wheel. "Paying attention is less important and is taken less seriously than it used to be," he says, "and that's very consequential for driving. The windshield is just another screen for some young people."[57] This attitude helps explain why many drivers, but especially young drivers, often ignore cell phone laws.

Is Addiction Defeating the Laws?

Another possible explanation for why cell phone laws have not reduced distracted driving is that many people have become addicted to their cell phones and simply cannot or will not put them away even when they are driving. People are reluctant to be apart from their phones, including while driving—even when it is against the law. In 2012 *Time* magazine surveyed five thousand people from the United States, the United Kingdom, Korea, China, India, South Africa, Indonesia, and Brazil about their cell phone use. The survey found that 25 percent checked their phone every thirty minutes, 20 percent checked every ten minutes, and 33 percent of respondents "admitted that being without their mobile for even short periods of time leaves them feeling anxious."[58]

Time journalist Nancy Gibbs notes that the bond between people and their cell phones is unlike anything in history: "It is hard to think of any tool, any instrument, any object in history with which so many developed so close a relationship so quickly as we have with our phones. Not the knife or match, the pen or page. Only money comes close—always at hand, don't leave home without it. But most of us don't take a wallet to bed with us, don't reach for it and check it every few minutes."[59]

With such a relationship, it is not surprising that more and more drivers are using cell phones, even when it is illegal. "I'm completely chained to my phone," says college student Marcie Gerhardt. "I try to be safer by taking it out of my purse and putting it on the seat next to me so I don't have to go digging in my purse if it rings. . . . I hear that little bongo drumbeat on my iPhone telling me I have a text coming in! And I can't resist looking at it right away."[60]

> "I hear that little bongo drumbeat on my iPhone telling me I have a text coming in! And I can't resist looking at it."[60]
>
> —Marcie Gerhardt, college student.

High-Tech Cars

Many researchers say that one of the most important reasons that the numbers of cell phone–related deaths and injuries continue to rise even though more laws are being passed probably has something to do with the cars themselves. Since the mid-2000s many cars have been equipped with hands-free technology such as Bluetooth that allows drivers to use their phones while keeping their hands on the steering wheel. Even newer technology is adding to the things a driver can do while behind the wheel. In 2012 many auto manufacturers began equipping cars with technology that allows drivers to be connected to the Internet so they can compose and check e-mail as well as access social network sites—all hands-free. Some cars even send e-mails to drivers when there is a change in driving conditions or if scheduled maintenance is due. All of these services—and more—are displayed on a colorful screen on the dashboard.

A Danger in Disguise

But while hands-free technology sounds safer than using a handheld phone, safety experts warn that this is not the case. In 2011 the AAA Foundation for Traffic Safety commissioned a study to learn whether hands-free cell phone technology was a safe alternative to handheld phones. The study, led by David Strayer, involved putting thirty-eight people in various driving situations while their levels of distraction

Parents and Multitasking

One of the most common reasons that laws alone will not solve the distracted driving problem is that motorists are chronic multitaskers. Teens are often criticized for multitasking while driving, but a study released in 2013 by the University of Michigan found that some parents are even worse.

Researchers interviewed more than six hundred parents of children between the ages of one and twelve. The parents were asked a range of questions about their use of cell phones while behind the wheel and also about other types of distractions. The study found that 90 percent of the parents admitted to technology-related multitasking in the last month—including talking on a cell phone, using a GPS, texting, and changing a DVD or CD—while driving.

were measured. The drivers had an average of almost seven years of driving experience.

The participants were asked to complete a series of driving tasks while they experienced distractions such as listening to the radio or talking with a passenger, talking on a handheld cell phone, talking on a hands-free system, and using the hands-free system to send and receive e-mails. The scientists used vehicles that were outfitted with cameras that tracked head and eye movement of the drivers. Specially designed caps worn by drivers allowed researchers to measure the amount of brain activity that was being used at any particular time during the test.

Hands Free—Distraction Free?

The results of the study, released in June 2013, helped scientists understand why laws alone have not made a difference in the numbers of deaths and injuries in cell phone–related accidents. The scientists found that talking on a hands-free cell phone was actually just as distracting as talking on a handheld cell phone. And using that hands-free device to send or respond to texts or e-mails was even more dangerous than using a regular cell phone.

Participants using hands-free phones showed dangerous mental distractions while driving. Although their eyes were on the road and their hands on the steering wheel, they were unable to react as quickly to important visual cues such as stop signs and pedestrians, even when those cues were directly in front of them. There was no significant difference between the inattention blindness resulting from the use of handheld or hands-free phones. "The assumption that . . . voice based interactions would be safe appears to be unwarranted," the study team writes. "Simply put, hands-free does not mean risk-free."[61]

In response to the study's findings, Robert L. Darbelnet, president of AAA, called on car manufacturers to slow their development of such communications systems. "There is a looming public safety crisis ahead with the future proliferation of these in-vehicle technologies," he announced. "It's time to consider limiting new and potentially dangerous mental distractions built into cars, particularly with the common public misperception that hands-free means risk-free."[62]

Some states prohibit drivers from using handheld cell phones but allow hands-free devices (pictured). Researchers say the use of hands-free phones by drivers is just as distracting and hazardous as the use of handheld phones.

Worry for the Future

Safety experts and researchers have expressed concern about the proliferation of cell phone use in cars. They acknowledge that the research proving the dangers of cell phone use is far outpacing the passage of laws that would limit or ban it. It is especially worrisome because there is a huge market for cars heavily equipped with hands-free technology.

Lawrence Gostin, a lawyer at Georgetown University, is concerned that states that have banned texting feel that they have already solved the distraction problem. As a result, they are not concerned with limiting or banning hands-free technology. "It sends a very bad message," he says, "that we don't take this very seriously."[63]

Other Efforts to Reduce Cell Phone Use by Drivers

Because laws alone cannot dissuade drivers from talking and texting on their cell phones while on the road, other efforts are being made to get drivers to change their habits. Attention-grabbing public service announcements, heart-wrenching public appearances by people involved in distracted driving crashes (both perpetrators and victims or their families), and technology are all part of the arsenal being deployed to encourage drivers to stop using cell phones while driving.

The Camera Does Not Lie

Most police departments have routinely used video cameras in their squad cars to protect both officers and civilians during traffic stops. In recent years, however, digital video cameras have proved especially effective in cases of drivers using cell phones. The reason, experts say, is that unlike the old video systems, the digital systems document not only the police stop but the crime itself.

The camera is mounted in the roof above the car's dashboard; from this vantage it captures everything the officer sees. It records constantly, feeding the images into a computer in the car. The moment the officer hits the siren and flashing lights, the system automatically begins to save the images being recorded plus up to about a minute or so of activity before that point. This creates a record not only of the traffic stop but also of the event that resulted in the stop.

Bradley Simonson credits the digital video camera in his patrol car with helping him catch cell phone–using drivers. Simonson says that he was recently sitting in his squad car at a busy intersection when he noticed a driver making the typical motions of someone using a cell phone: She looked at the road ahead of her, then down at her lap, then back at the road, and then he saw her raise the cell phone to her ear with her right hand while her left held the steering wheel. At that point he turned on his emergency lights to get her to pull over and stop. "So because [the camera] records back several seconds, even if she stops using her cell phone," he says, "the camera will have caught her using it seconds before she even sees my lights."[64]

The driver's response once she saw the police car's flashing lights behind her was also fairly typical, Simonson says. She immediately handed the phone to a child in the backseat. He continues: "When I stopped her, she first insisted that the phone was being used by the child, but I corrected her, saying that she didn't hand it off until she'd gone two more blocks. There was absolutely no way she could argue it. The judge could see the whole thing on the film, it was really clear, so that was that. Really, though, it would have been very hard to get a conviction without that camera."[65]

Looking Down on Texters

Many law enforcement officers would agree with Simonson that it is often difficult to catch motorists who are texting. As more and more research indicates how dangerous texting is, however, some new ideas are helping police catch more texting lawbreakers.

> "The judge could see the whole thing on the film, it was really clear, so that was that."[65]
>
> —Minneapolis police sergeant Bradley Simonson.

One idea that is taking hold in a number of states is the use of SUVs, which ride higher, and therefore give a police officer a better vantage point from which to spot texters. And because the cars are usually unmarked, motorists are unaware that they are being observed. SUVs are being used more and more in New York State since statistics showed that between 2005 and 2011, there was a 143 percent increase in cell phone–related crashes in the state.

The use of the unmarked SUVs proved to be a success. In 2012 the state issued 30,166 tickets for texting while driving—an increase of 234 percent from the year before. And New York police credit this to the use of the SUVs. "It's like taking candy from a baby,"[66] says New York State trooper Imani Kirkland.

A California Highway Patrol officer issues a citation to a motorist who was using a cell phone while driving. Many police departments have found video cameras mounted on patrol cars to be helpful as a tool for documenting cell phone use by drivers.

Preserving Incriminating Cell Phone Data

If law enforcement suspects that an accident resulting in deaths or serious injuries was caused by cell phone distraction, a police officer will often seize the driver's cell phone. "But I'm not permitted to scroll through it to see the calls or texts made on the phone without a search warrant," explains police officer Kevin Rofidal. "Not until a judge grants a search warrant can the phone be examined by law enforcement."[67]

However, keeping phone evidence safe while waiting for a judge to grant a search warrant could be problematic. There is technology available that enables a cell phone owner to wipe clean the phone's history in the event the phone is lost or stolen. "It is possible for the owner of that phone to wipe it," says forensic computer analyst David Lindman. "There are apps for certain cell phones that enable a customer to do what's called 'a remote wipe.' . . . You don't want a thief to get into your personal files or contacts."[68]

Apps to Discourage Distracted Driving

Though technology has been largely responsible for the rising numbers of cell phone–related accidents, it can also be a part of the solution. Some cell phone makers, as well as providers like Sprint and AT&T, have developed apps that promote safe driving habits.

For example, the Sprint app, known as Drive First, locks the phone when the car is traveling faster than 10 miles per hour (16 kph). When the phone is locked, incoming calls are transferred automatically to voice mail. The audio tones that usually alert users when they have incoming texts or e-mails are silenced, and auto replies explain to the caller that the person they called is driving and cannot reply.

Canary is an app designed by Apple especially for parents of young drivers. Using Canary, parents are able to monitor their teen's phone, getting alerts when the phone is going faster than 12 miles per hour (19 kph) or when the teen is texting while driving. Parents receive the alerts on their own phones or by e-mail.

Terry Solomon says she was a little hesitant at first to use an app on her daughter's phone. "I felt that it was kind of sneaky, monitoring my daughter's actions. Like I don't trust her. But I do—but I also know judgment isn't always great when you're 17. So I'd rather have her mad at me for a couple of days than have her injured or even killed due to a few seconds of bad decision-making when she's with her friends."

Terry Solomon, personal interview by author, September 28, 2013, Minneapolis, MN.

The same type of app could be used to remotely erase the text or call history from a confiscated phone before a warrant arrives. As a precaution, many police departments are using special evidence containers, called Faraday bags, when they seize a driver's phone. A Faraday bag looks like a thick bubble-wrapped envelope one might use to send something fragile through the mail. But the bags are layered with small amounts of nickel, tin, and silver. This material blocks the ability to remotely erase what could be important evidence.

Celebrities Speak Out

Technology is not the only tactic being tried in efforts to reduce distracted driving. Safety organizations have made a concerted effort to call attention to the issue. They have enlisted the help of celebrities such as musicians Tim McGraw and Justin Bieber and comedian Joel McHale to spread the message that cell phone use while driving is dangerous. In Bieber's public service announcement, the singer is shown walking along a road and is almost run down by a car loaded with teenage girls who are all texting on their cell phones. After the near miss, he walks over to their car and reminds them of the dangers of texting and driving.

Television personality Oprah Winfrey has also engaged in efforts to raise awareness of cell phone hazards on the road. In April 2010 Winfrey announced on her television show that a national No Phone Zone Day would be observed on April 30. Citing statistics about cell phone–caused accidents and introducing guests who had lost loved ones in accidents caused by cell phones, Winfrey urged her viewers to take a pledge vowing they would never text or talk on a cell phone while driving. "My biggest hope for the No Phone Zone campaign," she says, "is that it becomes mandatory that no one uses their phone in the car or texts while driving—just as seat belts are mandatory, just as driving while drunk is considered absolutely taboo. I'm hoping that this becomes not just law, but second nature for all of us."[69] In addition to the hundreds of thousands of viewers who signed Winfrey's online pledge, many celebrities also added their names—Jerry Seinfeld, Sandra Bullock, Morgan Freeman, Tina Fey, the cast of *Glee*, and Lady Antebellum among them.

Not Just Victims

Celebrities are not the only ones who are speaking out in an effort to raise awareness. Reggie Shaw, the young man whose texting while driving led to the 2006 deaths of two people in Utah, has been haunted by the tragic outcome of his actions. Before the accident, he says, he texted "close to 100 percent of the time" while driving. He wishes he had known more about the risks of texting while driving. "I just never thought about it," he said on a television interview. "Growing up, going to high school, going to driver's ed, it was never taught to me how dangerous it was."[70]

Since the crash Shaw has dedicated himself to spreading the word about how dangerous cell phone use can be. In 2013 he spoke at the National Organization for Youth Safety's Distracted Driving Summit about his experience. He has also done presentations at high schools, where he talks to students about the mistake he made and how the guilt and sadness have continued to eat away at him all these years since the crash. "This affects my life every day, It's something that I can never really forgive myself for. It was a poor choice that I made. I have trouble sleeping at night. You drive down the road, you see accidents on the side of the road, and instantly, that's the first thing that I think of. It's hard every day. It never gets easier."[71]

> "It was a poor choice that I made. I have trouble sleeping at night."[71]
>
> —Reggie Shaw, whose texting while driving caused the deaths of two people.

Shaw says that he sees in many high school students the same false sense of invincibility that he had as a teen driver. "A lot of them think along the lines like I thought: 'I can do this. I'm safe,'" he says. "I explain to them, 'It's not safe. Absolutely not. Look what it's done to me. Look what it's done to these two families. You don't want to put anyone through that. It's not worth it.'"[72]

A Film with Impact

Cell phone providers have a big stake in the safety of their customers. Aware of the fact that at least 10 percent of all crashes are caused by distracted driving (usually the distraction is a cell phone), AT&T, Verizon, Sprint, and T-Mobile approached award-winning filmmaker Werner Herzog to make a short film about the dangers of texting and driving.

The film, *From One Second to the Next*, is a series of interviews with people whose lives have been irrevocably changed due to cell phone–caused accidents. In one segment a young Indiana man named Chandler emotionally talks about how he killed three members of an Amish family in a horse-drawn buggy while he was texting. In another segment a mother talks about how life has changed for her family after a texting driver ran a stop sign and left her young son a paraplegic.

From Pain and Grief to Activism

One effective way of helping people understand the dangers of driving while using a cell phone is hearing the testimony of people who have been affected by it. Though it is emotionally draining and often visibly difficult for them, more and more people who have survived crashes caused by cell phone use are working hard to educate drivers about the risks of distracted driving.

One of these is Jacy Good, a young woman who was critically injured in a crash caused by a distracted driver. In May 2008 she and her parents were driving home from her college graduation in Allentown, Pennsylvania, when a motorist talking on his cell phone ran a red light. A semi on the other side of the road was forced to swerve, hitting the Goods' car head-on. Her parents were killed instantly, and Jacy spent two months in a coma. When she awoke, she had to learn to walk and talk again.

Today she needs a cane to walk and has the use of only one of her arms. She says she has turned her grief and anger into an effort to educate people about the horrific results of driving while using a cell phone. She also is working to get laws passed that ban cell phone use by drivers. She is determined that an accident like the one that shattered her life will not happen to another family. "If I can get laws passed," Jacy says, "my parents died for a reason."

Quoted in Nicole Weisensee, "A Tragic Crash, a Daughter's Crusade," *People*, April 11, 2011. www .people.com.

"I don't need to show blood and gore and wrecked cars," Herzog explained after finishing the film. "What I wanted to do was show the interior side of the catastrophes. . . . It's a deep raw emotion—the kind of deep wounds that are in those who were victims of accidents and also in those who were the perpetrators. Their life has changed and they are suffering forever. They have this sense of guilt that pervades every single action, every single day, every single dream and nightmare."[73]

Herzog says that he has received very positive feedback for his film. "The reaction is coming in . . . I mean hundreds of emails are coming in, parents writing to me. One teenage girl writes to me, 'I sat down [with] my mother and I told her, "You are texting when you're taking me to school; you are not going to do that again." My mother doesn't even take her cellphone with her [in the car] anymore.'"[74]

Learning Young

Police say that parents can be an important part of teaching their teens not to use cell phones while driving. "It's not the kind of teaching where you lecture your kids," says driving instructor Cynthia Dahl. "It's the kind where you teach by the example you set. If you text or talk while driving, why exactly would you think your kids would take you seriously when you tell them not to do it?"[75]

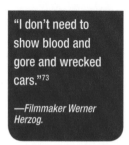

"I don't need to show blood and gore and wrecked cars."[73]

—Filmmaker Werner Herzog.

Simonson says that though teenagers and cell phones are often inseparable, it is not unreasonable for parents to remind them about the dangers of cell phone use while driving. "Teenagers have phones—I get that," he says, "but I tell my kids not to have theirs on in the car. If it rings, don't answer, if you absolutely have to, pull over. If I call my daughter on her cell, the first thing I ask is, 'Are you driving right now?' I don't want to start a conversation with her while she's behind the wheel. She's heard all this already, but I feel better just making sure she hears it again. And every once in awhile, I'll jump in the car with her, just to make sure she's remembering this stuff."[76]

David Melton, a director at the Liberty Mutual Research Institute for Safety, says that kind of parental interest is valuable. It also helps for parents to look at their phone bills to get an idea of how often their teens are texting. If the records indicate that they text often, it is a good idea to remind them frequently about the no-texting rule while on the road. "Young kids have seen us exhibit bad behaviors," Melton said. "No matter what we tell them about safe driving how can they believe we're serious about it? We must become good examples. Teens get safe driving examples from many sources but no one more than mom or dad."[77]

Self-Driving Cars?

The allure of technology has been a major cause of the problem of drivers' cell phone use. Research has proved that talking, texting, and

High school students in New Mexico sign a no-texting pledge in 2013 as part of AT&T's It Can Wait campaign. The company is one of several cell service providers involved in public education efforts aimed at reducing distracted driving.

sending or reading e-mail while driving can have disastrous results. However, many experts believe that banning phones—hands-free or otherwise—is not practical. "History has taught us you can't turn back the clock on technology—the solutions have to come from the next step. I really don't think it's going to get solved by passing more laws, or by writing more tickets,"[78] says Eric Roeske.

Some believe that next step might be technology that lessens the risks of driving and cell phone use by eliminating the driver. The search engine giant Google is already testing driverless cars. Google engineers have tested self-driving cars on more than 200,000 miles (321,869 km) of highways in Nevada and California. By using a combination of lasers, radar, and cameras, the vehicles are able to analyze and process information far faster than a human being can.

Remarkably, in some of the Google tests the cars were able to learn the details of a road simply by driving on it several times: "When it was time to drive itself," notes Christopher Neiger of the website HowStuffWorks, "it was able to identify when there were pedestrians crossing and stopped to let them pass by. Self-driving cars could make transportation safer for all of us by eliminating the cause of 95 percent of today's accidents: human error."[79]

> "I don't think it will be solved by passing more laws, or by writing more tickets."[78]
>
> —Minnesota State Patrol lieutenant Eric Roeske.

In the meantime, however, individuals will have to take responsibility for their own safe driving. With the mass of research proving the dangers of cell phone use by drivers, experts such as David Strayer hope that even without self-driving cars, driving and cell phone use will be universally recognized in the future as a foolish combination. "We might actually look back and say, 'Well *that* was really stupid,'" he says. "But I don't know if that's going to happen."[80]

Source Notes

Introduction: Cell Phones Behind the Wheel

1. Quoted in Shelby Capacio and Leah Beno, "Police: Byron Teen Killed in Crash on First Day of School Was Texting," Fox 9.com. www.myfoxtwincities.com.

2. Mike Duffy, telephone interview by author, August 2013.

3. Quoted in Capacio and Beno, "Police: Byron Teen Killed in Crash on First Day of School Was Texting."

4. Moira Evans, telephone interview by author, August 18, 2013.

5. Quoted in Capacio and Beno, "Police: Byron Teen Killed in Crash on First Day of School Was Texting."

Chapter One: The Distractions of Driving

6. Eric Roeske, personal interview by author, St. Paul, MN, August 6, 2013.

7. Bradley Simonson, personal interview by author, Minneapolis, MN, July 18, 2013.

8. Carley Schwartz, personal interview by author, Minneapolis, MN, July 5, 2013.

9. Schwartz, personal interview.

10. Matt Richtel, "Digital Billboards, Diversions Drivers Can't Escape," *New York Times*, March 1, 2010.

11. Richtel, "Digital Billboards, Diversions Drivers Can't Escape."

12. Caaqil Iqbal, personal interview by author, Minneapolis, MN, August 3, 2013.

13. Kevin Rofidal, personal interview by author, Edina, MN, July 23, 2013.

14. Roeske, personal interview.

15. Roeske, personal interview.

16. Quoted in *From One Second to the Next*, documentary, directed by Werner Herzog. www.youtube.com/watch?v=_BqFkRwdFZ0.

17. Quoted in Paige Lampson, "Moment of Impact: GHS Students Become Educated on How to Avoid Accidents." www.galtherald online.com.

18. Quoted in Larry Copeland, "Texting in Traffic: Adults Worse than Teens," *USA Today*, March 28, 2013. www.usatoday.com.

19. Kathleen, telephone interview by author, September 1, 2013.

20. Quoted in Britney Fitzgerald, "Chance Bothe Texts: 'I Need to Quit Texting' Before Near-Deadly Truck Crash," *Huffington Post*, August 2, 2012. www.huffingtonpost.com.

21. Quoted in Fitzgerald, "Chance Bothe Texts."

22. Quoted in Karl Penhaul, Laura Smith-Spark, and Laura Perez Maestro, "Driver Detained as Investigators Probe Spain Train Crash," CNN, July 26, 2013. www.cnn.com.

Chapter Two: The Science of Distraction

23. Arthur Wouters, telephone interview by author, September 19, 2013.

24. Nathan Seppa, "Impactful Distraction: Talking While Driving Poses Dangers That People Seem Unable to See," *Science News*, August 9, 2013. www.sciencenews.org.

25. Quoted in YouTube, "Intel Labs Measure Cognitive Workload of Distracted Drivers," June 26, 2013. www.youtube.com.

26. Quoted in YouTube, "Inattentional Blindness, Gorilla in the Court." www.youtube.com.

27. Quoted in YouTube, "Inattentional Blindness, Gorilla in the Court."

28. Jim Lutz, personal interview by author, Minneapolis, MN, August 29, 2013.

29. Lutz, personal interview.

30. Quoted in Leslie Shepherd, "Research Finds Brain Can't Cope with Making a Left-Hand Turn and Talking on Hands-Free Phone at the Same Time," Newsroom, St. Michael's Hospital, February 28, 2013. www.stmichaelshospital.com.

31. Quoted in Oprah.com, "Distracted Driving: What You Don't See," January 15, 2010 www.oprah.com.

32. Quoted in U News Center, "Frequent Multitaskers Are Bad at It," news release, University of Utah, January 23, 2013. http://unews .utah.edu.

Chapter Three: Cell Phones and the Law

33. Lee Raine, "Cell Phone Ownership Hits 91% of Adults," Pew Research Center, June 6, 2013. www.pewresearch.org.

34. Louisa McIntyre, personal interview by author, Richfield, MN, September 4, 2013.

35. Marcie Rivera, personal interview by author, St. Paul, MN, August 12, 2013.

36. Mike Pfiefer, telephone interview by author, August 3, 2013.

37. Quoted in Oprah.com, "Oprah's No-Texting Campaign," January 15, 2010. www.oprah.com.

38. Quoted in Oprah.com, "Oprah's No-Texting Campaign."

39. Quoted in John Ingold, "Colorado Criminalizes Texting, Tweeting While Driving," *Denver Post*, June 2, 2009. www.denverpost .com.

40. Quoted in *Huffington Post*, "Taylor Sauer Died While Driving and Facebooking: Now Parents Want to Make It Illegal," March 5, 2012. www.huffingtonpost.com.

41. Quoted in *Huffington Post*, "Taylor Sauer Died While Driving and Facebooking."

42. Quoted in Your4State.com, "New Laws Take Effect and Crack Down on Distracted Driving," July 1, 2013. www.your4state.com.

43. Quoted in Hang Up and Drive, "Cell Phone Use While Driving May Soon Be Illegal Statewide in Illinois," August 15, 2013. http://hangupanddrive.com.

44. Quoted in *Alaska Native News* (Homer, AK), "It's Official: Texting While Driving Is Illegal in Alaska," May 10, 2012. http://alaska-native-news.com.

45. Quoted in Howard Fischer, "Brewer Dislikes Driver-Texting Ban," *Arizona Business Gazette* (Phoenix), June 17, 2010. www.azcentral.com.

46. Quoted in Rebecca McKinsey, "Driver-Texting Ban Still Elusive in Arizona," *Arizona Republic* (Phoenix), AZ Central.com, August 2, 2013. www.azcentral.com.

47. Quoted in McKinsey, "Driver-Texting Ban Still Elusive in Arizona."

48. Quoted in US Department of Transportation, "U.S. Transportation Secretary LaHood Announces Final Rule That Bans Hand-Held Cell Phone Use by Drivers of Buses and Large Trucks," news release, November 23, 2001. www.fmcsa.dot.gov.

49. Quoted in WREX News, "Local Truck Drivers React to Proposed Ban on Cell Phones," September 14, 2011. www.wrex.com.

50. Quoted in Kevin Short, "Spain Train Crash Shows Importance of Taking Distracted Driving Seriously," *Huffington Post*, August 2, 2013. www.huffingtonpost.com.

Chapter Four: Have Laws Reduced Cell Phone Distraction?

51. Quoted in *NSC News*, "Recent Analysis Indicates Cell Phone Distracted Driving Crashes Vastly Under-Reported," May 7, 2013. www.nsc.org.

52. Simonson, personal interview.

53. Quoted in Mark Bowes, "Virginia Texting While Driving Ban Goes into Effect, Amidst Concerns About Enforcement," *Huffington Post*, June 30, 2013. www.huffingtonpost.com.

54. Quoted in Bowes, "Virginia Texting While Driving Ban Goes into Effect."

55. Jeff Chaney, personal interview by author, August 21, 2013.

56. Quoted in Seppa, "Impactful Distraction."

57. Quoted in Seppa, "Impactful Distraction."

58. Nancy Gibbs, "Your Life Is Fully Mobile," *Time*, August 16, 2012. http://techland.time.com.

59. Gibbs, "Your Life Is Fully Mobile."

60. Marcie Gerhardt, telephone interview by author, September 11, 2013.

61. Quoted in Eryn Brown, "AAA Study on Cell Phones in Cars: 'Hands Free Is Not Risk-Free,'" *Los Angeles Times*, June 12, 2013. http://articles.latimes.com.

62. Quoted in Brown, "AAA Study on Cell Phones in Cars."

63. Quoted in Seppa, "Impactful Distractions."

Chapter Five: Other Efforts to Reduce Cell Phone Use by Drivers

64. Simonson, personal interview.

65. Simonson, personal interview.

66. Quoted in Kevin Short, "New York State Troopers Battle Texting While Driving, Cell Phone Use on the Roads," *Huffington Post*, July 23, 2013. www.huffingtonpost.com.

67. Rofidal, personal interview.

68. David Lindman, personal interview by author, July 23, 2013.

69. Quoted in Christine Bude Nyholm, "Oprah Winfrey Asks Guests and Viewers to Sign No Phone Zone Pledge," Yahoo! Voices, May 3, 2010. http://voices.yahoo.com.

70. Quoted in CNN, "Oprah: Stay Off Your Phone While Driving," January 20, 2010. www.cnn.com.

71. Quoted in CNN, "Oprah: Stay Off Your Phone While Driving."

72. Quoted in CNN, "Oprah: Stay Off Your Phone While Driving."

73. Quoted in *All Tech Considered*, "Herzog Plumbs Guilt and Loss Wrought by Texting and Driving," NPR, August 16, 2013. www.npr.org.

74. Quoted in *All Tech Considered*, "Herzog Plumbs Guilt and Loss Wrought by Texting and Driving."

75. Cynthia Dahl, telephone interview by author, September 3, 2013.

76. Simonson, personal interview.

77. Quoted in Randy Craig, "Texting While Driving: Parents' Role in Prevention," National PTA. www.pta.org.

78. Roeske, personal interview.

79. Christopher Neiger, "5 Future Car Technologies That Truly Have a Chance," HowStuffWorks. http://auto.howstuffworks.com.

80. Quoted in Seppa, "Impactful Distractions."

Related Organizations and Websites

Cell Phone Safety

website: www.cellphonesafety.org

This site was created by the National Consumer Advocacy Commission, an organization that works to educate cell phone users on a number of issues, including the dangers of driving while using a cell phone.

Don't Drive and Text

222 N. Main St., Suite A
Bryan, TX 77803
website: http://dontdriveandtext.org

This organization works to educate consumers on the dangers of texting and driving, providing statistical information as well as showing dramatic video testimonies of friends and families of victims of distracted driving.

FocusDriven

PO Box 2262
Grapevine, TX 76099
website: www.focusdriven.org

This organization supports victims of cell phone–distracted driving and the families of victims, and works to increase public awareness of the dangers. In addition, FocusDriven promotes public policies that will help solve the problem.

National Highway Traffic Safety Administration (NHTSA)

1200 New Jersey Ave. SE
Washington, DC 20590
website: www.nhtsa.gov

Established in 1970, the NHTSA is dedicated to achieving the highest standards of safety on the nation's highways. In addition to promoting safe driving practices for all drivers, it targets teen drivers to avoid dangers such as drunk driving, nonuse of seatbelts, and driving while using cell phones.

National Safety Council (NSC)
1121 Spring Lake Dr.
Itasca, IL 60143
website: www.nsc.org

The NSC is dedicated to saving lives by preventing accidents that can result in injuries and deaths at work, in homes, and on the nation's roads. The NSC partners with elected officials, businesses, and the public in order to decrease distracted driving by providing information to teens and parents on how to avoid the use of cell phones while behind the wheel.

Pew Research Center
1615 L St. NW, Suite 700
Washington, DC 20036
website: info@pewresearch.org

This is a nonpartisan research organization that conducts and analyzes the results of public opinion polls and demographic studies on a variety of issues and trends, including the growing concern about the dangers of cell phone use by drivers.

Text Free Driving Organization
website: www.textfreedriving.org

This Florida organization is working to make highways, roads, and neighborhood streets safer by promoting legislation that would eliminate the use of cell phones by drivers.

Advocates of Highway and Auto Safety

750 First St. NE, Suite 901
Washington, DC 20002
website: www.saferoads.org

This organization is an alliance of consumer, medical, public health, and safety groups, and insurance companies and agents working to make America's roads safer. The AHAS supports bills that will increase the number of states with cell phone laws to ultimately reduce the number of deaths and injuries associated with distracted driving.

Governors Highway Safety Organization

444 N. Capitol St., NW, Suite 722
Washington, DC 20001
website: headquarters@ghsa.org

The GHSA represents the state and territorial safety offices that implement programs that address behavioral highway safety issues, including impaired and distracted driving. The organization advocates and provides leadership for states to improve traffic safety and influence national laws and policies.

Books

Sylvia Engdahl, *Electronic Devices*. Farmington Hills, MI: Greenhaven, 2012.

Stefan Kiesbye, ed., *Cell Phones and Driving*. Farmington Hills, MI: Greenhaven, 2011.

Stefan Kiesbye, ed., *Distracted Driving*. Farmington Hills, MI: Greenhaven, 2012.

Carla Mooney, *Thinking Critically: Cell Phones*. San Diego, CA: ReferencePoint, 2014.

Patricia D. Netzley, *How Does Cell Phone Use Impact Teenagers?* San Diego, CA: ReferencePoint, 2013.

Bonnie Szumski and Jill Karson, *Are Cell Phones Dangerous?* San Diego, CA: ReferencePoint, 2011.

Internet Sources

AAA Foundation for Safety, "Cognitive Distraction: Something to Think About," June 10, 2013. www.aaafoundation.org/cognitive-dis traction-something-think-about.

Lynette Adams, "Hang Up and Drive: Jacy Good Advocates for Cell-Free Roads," WHEC Rochester, February 15, 2013. www.whec.com /news/stories/S2933348.shtml?cat=565.

Daniel Bean, "Drivers Know Cellphone Use Dangerous, but Drive and Phone Anyway," ABC News, April 6, 2013. http://abcnews.go.com /Technology/drivers-cell-dangerous-drive/story?id=18890675.

Ken Leiser, "Feds Want Ban on Cellphones While Driving After Missouri Pileup," *St. Louis Post-Dispatch*, December 14, 2011. www .stltoday.com/news/local/govt-and-politics/feds-want-ban-on -cellphones-while-driving-after-missouri-pileup/article_45bdf5f5 -0576-5633-adea-dd76ece9ffad.html.

Byron Spice, "Carnegie Mellon Study Shows Just Listening to Cell Phones Significantly Impairs Drivers," Carnegie Mellon University, March 5, 2008. www.cmu.edu/news/archive/2008/March/march5 _drivingwhilelistening.shtml.

University of Utah News, "Frequent Multitaskers Are Bad at It," January 23, 2013. http://unews.utah.edu/news_releases/frequent -mulitaskers-are-bad-at-it.

Index

Note: Boldface page numbers indicate illustrations.

American Automobile Association (AAA), 47, 49
Amo, Francisco Jose Garzon, 18–19
Atchley, Richard, 48
AT&T, 15

Best, Kyle, 37
Bieber, Justin, 57
Bothe, Chance, 16
brain
  occipital/parietal lobes of, 26–27, 28
  research on distracted driving and, 21–23
Brewer, Jan, 38
Burleson, Nate, 15

cameras, on police cars, 53–54
Canary (app), 56
Carnegie Mellon University, 26
cars
  falling objects in, 15
  hands-free technology in, 49
    risk of, 50–51
  self-driving, 60–62

cell phone(s)
  addiction to, 48–49
  apps for, to prevent distracted driving, 56
  evidence of commercial bus driver using, 18
  percentage of adults/teens using, 32
  use while driving, prevalence of, 15, 30
Centers for Disease Control and Prevention (CDC), 14, 30
Chabris, Chris, 23
Chaney, Jeff, 47
Colonna, Shannon, 37
Colorado, ban on cell phone use by drivers in, 35
commercial vehicles, crashes caused by distracted drivers of, 16–19
conversations, passenger *vs.* cell phone, levels of distraction from, 27
Crawford, Paul, 21, 22, 23

Dahl, Cynthia, 60
Dailey, Misty, 14
D'Amico, John, 38
Darbelnet, Robert L., 51
deaths

from cell phone use by drivers,
8
    underreporting of, 43–44
  from distracted driving, 14, 43
Dewniak, Debbie, 14
digital billboards, 10–11
"Digital Billboards, Diversions
  Drivers Can't Escape"
  (Richtel), 10
distracted driving
  apps to discourage, 56
  causes of, 9–13
  See also prevention
Drive First (app), 56
driving distractions
  cognitive, 12–13
  falling objects in car, 15
  from hands-free technology,
    50–51
  levels of, from passenger *vs.*
    cell phone conversations, 27
  number of deaths caused by,
    14, 43
  physical, 11–12
  visual, 9–10
    from outside of vehicle,
      10–11
drunk driving, 57
  likelihood of traffic accident
    from, *vs.* cell phone chat, 29
  prevalence among teens, 30

Eisenbiess, Andres, 41
Evans, Moira, 8

falling objects, in car, 15
Faraday bags, 56

Farley, Steve, 39
Fatal Analysis Reporting System
  (National Highway Traffic
  Safety Administration),
  43–44
Federal Railroad Administration
  (FRA), 41
Forney, Erica, 34–35
Forney, Shelly, 35
Foundation for Traffic Safety
  (American Automobile
  Association), 47, 49, 51
Froetscher, Janet, 44
From One Second to the Next
  (film), 58–59
functional near-infrared (fNIR)
  spectrometer, 21
Furaro, James, 36

Gara, Les, 38
Gerhardt, Marcie, 49
Gibbs, Nancy, 48–49
Godfrey, Alan, 17
Good, Jacy, 59
Google, 61–62
Gosnell, Warren, 37
Gostin, Lawrence, 52
Governors Highway Safety
  Association (GHSA), 43

Herzog, Werner, 58, 59

Idaho, ban on cell phone use by
  drivers in, 35–36
inattention blindness, 23, 25
invincibility, drivers' sense of,
  47–48

"The Invisible Gorilla"
  experiment, 23–24
Iqbal, Caaqil, 11
It Can Wait campaign (AT&T),
  61

Just, Marcel, 26, 28

Kelley, Sheldon, 35
Kirkland, Imani, 54
Kubert, David, 37
Kubert, Linda, 37

LaHood, Ray, 40–41
Lake, Charlene, 15, 16
laws, banning cell phone use
  while driving
  confusion about, 45–47
  difficulty in enforcement of,
    44–45
  federal, 40–41
  hands-free technology and, 52
  number of states with, 43
  resistance to, 32–33, 38, 41
  variation between states on, 33
Lindman, David, 55
Logan, Deianerah, 6–7
Logan, Matt, 6–7, 8
Logan, Megan, 6–7, 8
Lutz, Jim, 25

magnetic resonance imaging
  (MRI), 25–26
McGraw, Tim, 57
McHale, Joel, 57
McIntyre, Louisa, 32

Melton, David, 60
Moriarty, Paul D., 39
multitasking, while driving
  prevalence of, among parents,
    50
  students' perceived ability in,
    29–31

Nass, Clifford, 27, 48
National Highway Traffic Safety
  Administration (NHTSA), 8,
  14, 43
Neiger, Christopher, 62
New York Times (newspaper), 43
Nikki's Law (NJ), 39

occipital lobe, 26–27, 28
O'Connell, Jemma, 17
O'Dell, Keith, 36
Olsen, Emily, 30
Onwudinjo, Miki, 18
Operation Span (OSPAN) test,
  30–31
opinion polls. *See* surveys

parents
  prevalence of multitasking
    while driving among, 50
  role in preventing distracted
    driving, 60
parietal lobe, 26–27, 28
Pew Research, 32
Pfiefer, Mike, 33
polls. *See* surveys
prevention
  efforts of celebrities in, 57

role of parents in, 60

railroad engineers
   train crash in Spain caused by
     texting by, 17, 17–19
   US ban on cell phone use by,
     41–42
Richtel, Matt, 10–11
Ritter, Bill, 35
Roeske, Eric, 9, 13, 61, 62
Rofidal, Kevin, 11–12, 55

Sanbonmatsu, David, 29, 30,
  31
Sanchez, Robert, 41
Sauer, Clay, 36
Sauer, Shauna, 36
Sauer, Taylor, 35–36
Schwartz, Carley, 9–10, 11
Schweizer, Tom, 25, 26
Science News (magazine), 21
Shaw, Reggie, 36, 57–58
Sheldon, Greg, 45
Simon, Dan, 23
Simonson, Bradley, 9, 44–45, 47,
  53–54, 60
Solomon, Terry, 56
Sorce, Vinnie, 39–40
Strayer, David, 29, 30, 49, 62
Stubbs, Stacey, 40
surveys
   on awareness of dangers of
     texting while driving, 47
   on cell phone use, 48
   on eating/drinking while
     driving, 11

   of parents, on multitasking
     while driving, 50
   on prevalence of texting by
     adults, 15
   of teenagers, on risky driving
     behaviors, 30
Swedish Transport
  Administration, 11
Szabo, Joseph, 41–42

Taylor's Law (ID), 35–36
teenagers
   percentage reporting risky
     driving behaviors, 30
   percentage reporting texting
     while driving, 15
   percentage using cell phones,
     32
texting
   of person driving car, liability
     for, 37
   while driving
     awareness of dangers of, 47
     dangers of, 14
     prevalence among teenage
      drivers, 30
     prevalence of, by adults *vs.*
      teens, 15
Time (magazine), 48
traffic accidents
   from distracted driving,
     underreporting of, 43–44
   likelihood of, from cell phone
     chat *vs.* drunk driving, 29
   percentage with cell phone as
     factor, 8, 14

train crashes
  in Chatsworth, CA (2008),
    41
  in Santiago de Compostela,
    Spain (2013), 17, 17–19
trucking industry, opposition of,
  to cell phone bans, 41
Tyson, Greg, 46–47

University of Leeds, 11
University of Madrid, 20

Utah, ban on cell phone use by
  drivers in, 36–37

vehicles, heavy, accidents caused
  by distracted drivers of, 16–19
Virginia, law on cell phone use
  by drivers in, 45–46

Winfrey, Oprah, 57
Wiseman, Richard, 23, 24
Wouters, Arthur, 20

About the Author

Gail B. Stewart is an award-winning author of more than 250 books for children, teens, and young adults. She lives with her husband in Minneapolis and is the mother of three grown sons.